W9-CTI-406

DEPTH ◆ IRIDESCENCE ◆ LUMINOSITY ◆ LUSTER ◆ OPALESCENCE ◆ TRANSPARENCY

The Magical Effects *of* Color

BY JOEN WOLFROM

C&T PUBLISHING

The Magical Effects of Color
Copyright © 1992 Joen Wolfrom

Cover Art:
Sunset (*airbrushed art for front and back cover backgrounds*) 1992
by Victoria Thompson, 763 Kearny Way, Napa, California 94559

Front: Tripping Around the World in a Splash of Color (1992), Owner: Danielle Wolfrom
Back: Dreaming of . . . A Room of My Own (1991)
by Joen Wolfrom

Editor: Diane Pedersen
Copy Editor: Judith M. Moretz
Design & Art Director: Diana L. Grinwis
          Grinwis Art Service, P. O. Box 6062, East Lansing, Michigan 48826-6062
Color Illustration: Judith Prowse Buskirk
          Gig Harbor, Washington
Innovative Perspective Drawings by Larry Barger
Computer Illustration: Chrysteen & Craig Diskowski
          Edge Design, Campbell, California
Line Art Illustration: Kathryn Darnell
          Darnell Calligraphy & Illustration, 210 Abbott Rd, Studio 40, East Lansing, Michigan 48823
Principal Photographer: Ken Wagner
          Wagner Photo Lab, 82 S. Main, Seattle, Washington 98104

Published by
C & T Publishing
P.O. Box 1456
Lafayette, California 94549

ISBN 0-914881-53-1

Library of Congress Catalog Card No: 92-53800

Library of Congress Cataloging-in-Publication Data

Wolfrom, Joen.
     The magical effects of color / Joen Wolfrom.
               p.   cm.
     Includes bibliographical references and index.
     ISBN 0-914881-53-1 : $19.95
     1. Quilts–Technique. 2. Quilts–Patterns. 3. Color in textile crafts.
4. Visual perception. 5. Isometric projection. I. Title.
NK9104.W66 1992
746.9'7–dc20   92-53800
                    CIP

Pantone is a registered trademark of Pantone, Inc.
Liquitex Acrylic is a registered trademark of Binney & Smith, Inc.

Printed in Hong Kong by Regent Publishing Services Ltd.
2   3   4   5   6   7   8   9   10

We wish to thank the following publishers for permission
to use excerpts from works in copyright:

Editions d'Art Albert Skira S. A., Geneva ©1986.
Portraits et Confidences by Pascal Bonafoux.

Paul Hamlyn Publishing Group, Limited,
a part of Reed International Books, London ©1980.
The Impressionists by Denis Thomas.

Harvard University Press, Cambridge, Massachusetts ©1963.
The Shape of Content by Ben Shahn.

Watson-Guptil Publications, a division
of BPI Communications, New York ©1983.
Drawing With Color and Imagination by Gaspare DeFiore.

The Magical Effects Of Color

Acknowledgments

It has been a wonderful experience working with the C&T Publishing family during the writing of *The Magical Effects of Color*. I am deeply appreciative of Tom, Carolie, Tony, and Todd Hensley for their great support and enthusiasm for this book.

Because *The Magical Effects of Color* itself is an example of individual creativity and artistic expression, I am especially grateful to Todd Hensley, president of C&T, and editor Diane Pedersen for the opportunity to pursue this project. Not only did they give me the freedom to create the book I had envisioned, they also allowed me to write it in my own style. I also wish to thank Diane for her thoughtful comments and suggestions. It was a joy working with someone whose excitement about this project equalled my own.

Additionally, I wish to give special thanks to graphic designer Diana Grinwis and copy editor Judith Moretz. Both contributed immensely to the visual quality and readability of *The Magical Effects of Color*. They, along with Kathryn Darnell and Rose Sheifer, have combined their technical skills and unique talents so that this book could be presented in the best possible format.

I wish to pay tribute to Ken Wagner, a photographer from Seattle, Washington. His work is unsurpassed in the field of product photography and his talents have been well utilized in creating the color section of this book. Ken's patience, untiring efforts, and excellent technical abilities have brought to this book exquisite color visions of beautiful works of art.

Thanks also goes to Judith Prowse Buskirk, whose wonderful color illustrations have been included to clarify many of the concepts addressed in this book. I am particularly grateful to Judith for taking on this assignment when I was unable to do the illustrations because of an untimely hand injury. Her work has added much to the presentation of the color concepts.

It was a great pleasure to work with Victoria Thompson, the talented artist whose background art was included on the book's cover. Additionally, I wish to thank Martie Huston, Judy Dales, and Pat Magaret for their extra efforts and long hours of creative work. Also, thanks goes to Marie Anderson, a retired fine-dressmaking instructor from Bates Technical Institute in Tacoma, who so generously shared with me her fabric knowledge and technical sewing skills. Her four years of instruction has given me a solid foundation to use in the quilting field.

For thoughtful suggestions, friendship, and laughter along the intense road of writing, I thank my dear friends Elly Sienkiewicz, Janice Richards, and Connie Snell. It is an honor and a pleasure to include many of my friends' and colleagues' art in this book. I was thrilled that they so willingly wished to share the results of their own creative expression and wonderful talent. Some contributors created art especially for *The Magical Effects of Color*, while others had existing pieces that fit beautifully with the concepts presented here. To all of these contributing artists, a special thanks is given. This book could never have been so visually successful without your beautiful creations. I am spellbound by your talents and pleased with your generous spirit. May you continue in your many creative successes.

I thank you all: Charlotte Andersen, Joy Baaklini, Diane Basch, Patty Bentley, Nancy Billings, Nancy Breland, Judy Dales, Sarah Dickson, Joan Dyer, Caryl Fallert, Virginia Freal, Geraldine Gahan, Alison Goss, Rosemarie Guttler, Nancy Halpern, Karla Harris, Martie Huston, Suzanne Kjelland, Friederike Kohlhaussen, Pat Magaret, Marian Marias, Grania McElligott, Maureen McGee, Evelyn Montague, Mary Morgan, Miriam Nathan-Roberts, Joy Nixon, Regula Nussbaumer, Erika Odemer, Karen Perrine, Shirley Perryman, Cheryl Phillips, Katerine Picot, Laura Reinstattler, Janice Richards, Amanda Richardson, Carol Rothrock, Rita Scannell, Judy Sogn, Eileen Sullivan, Judith Tinkl, Carol Ann Wadley, Lassie Wittman, Martha Woodworth, and Jason Yenter.

I also wish to thank conference sponsors, organization members, educational faculties, and editors who have invited me to teach, lecture, write, and share my ideas and knowledge. As well, I am filled with gratitude for the individuals who have participated in these activities over the years. I am overwhelmed by your wonderful support, encouragement, and friendship. It is because of you, and for you, that this book has been written.

This book is dedicated

To
Sally Herron,
Fauntleroy Elementary School,
an unforgettable fifth grade teacher who taught me
almost everything I have needed to know
about the English language.

To
Francis Aranyi,
founder and foremost conductor of the Seattle Youth Symphony,
a taskmaster who knew the meaning of discipline and hard work.
His unyielding commitment and dedication to music
enticed a generation of youth to accomplish incredible feats.
A solo flute plays no more,
but music lives in the heart forever.

To
John Knox,
Sealth High School,
a journalism teacher who took an enormous risk
by going against tradition
when he appointed his first female editor,
thus providing me with priceless experiences
and countless rewards.

To
Larry Lawrence,
Central Washington University,
an English professor whose reputation decreed
that only the serious writers walk through his door.
I dared to take the challenge, finding a most memorable teacher
who demanded that I live up to his expectations.

I give thanks to
these outstanding educators and countless others
who have dedicated their lives to youth.
Their combined guidance, inspiration, and knowledge
have helped give me a strong foundation
so that I might seek to find my own talents
and make my own personal commitments and contributions
to my family, community, and profession.

May there always be individuals who make a difference.

The Quest

My entrance into the art world began unceremoniously and without intent. I became interested in quiltmaking in the early 1970s when I needed an outside activity to stimulate my mind after leaving my profession to become a full-time mother and homemaker. To a layman like myself, there was no indication that a relationship between quiltmaking and art existed; it was a craft that embraced strong traditions and well-preserved techniques. Quiltmaking seemed like a safe and understandable activity for someone who had years of sewing experience.

Unfortunately, I was dissatisfied with the visual outcome of nearly all my early projects. I simply could not achieve the results I yearned to capture. Nor could I figure out how to execute the visual beauty that danced elusively in my mind. Eventually I realized there were two major elements to quiltmaking: the technical aspects of physically making the quilt, and the artistic principles for creating a visually beautiful design. Creating a technically perfect quilt did not guarantee visual beauty. Instead, each element enhanced the other's position; but neither could compensate for a lack in the other. Sadly, I could find no resource to answer my numerous questions about the issues that most concerned me—those of color, fabric selection, design, and visual illusions.

Some years later, when I began looking at the world around me in more than a cursory manner, I found to my surprise that nature provided clues to the mysteries of color, illusions, and design. Incredulously, I attained my first real understanding of afterimages and luminosity from gazing at sunsets. I then began seriously analyzing sunsets and sunrises, skies, water, clouds, flowers, and other natural elements, wondering if their qualities could be translated into color theory—and then perhaps duplicated through fabric manipulation. To my amazement, I found that I could learn wonderful color concepts from nature. Additionally, the same effects could be created in art by following nature's lead.

Awakened to the possibility that nature could provide answers to my many color questions, I began observing, experimenting, researching, and evaluating, using nature as my primary mentor. Through my studies, nature has shown me how colors can be organized and how they can interact with each other, both subtly and dramatically. Nature has also provided me with more than the basics by illustrating in numerous ways how to create wonderful illusions such as depth, luster, reflection, and luminosity. In all, working with color has led to fascinating discoveries.

I have included many of these observations and findings in *The Magical Effects of Color*. The desire for such information is overwhelmingly apparent from the wide interest shown for learning these concepts not only by those who enroll in classes, but by the number of people who make inquiries about color workshops. Because my primary interest lies within the world of quilt and textile art, I have included specific information for those who work in fabric, although much of this is also relevant to artists of other mediums. These special features include: (1) guidelines for creating successful designs; (2) suggestions for promoting creative growth; (3) suggestions for selecting appropriate fabric; (4) traditional and contemporary quilt/patchwork designs related to the concepts addressed; (5) ideas for enhancing designs with quilting lines; and (6) instructions for beginning pattern drafting.

I have enjoyed writing about the many fascinating aspects of art and nature that have piqued my curiosity and challenged my senses. I hope *The Magical Effects of Color* will offer people from all backgrounds, mediums, and levels of experience the opportunity to learn, in a comprehensive yet nonthreatening way, how to unlock many of the mysteries in the world of artistic expression. May this book provide you with a firm foundation, so that you can capture the emotive effects of color and create wondrous illusionary qualities in your art. Read and enjoy!

Joen

Commencement

We each have our own sensitivity to beauty, color, and creative imagery. This area of our life is highly personal. The designs that appeal to us, the way we strive to put colors together, the textures we choose—there are no rights or wrongs. Whether we are moved by the abstract or deeply touched by realistic representation is an individual choice. And in making this choice it is nearly impossible to isolate color, as it is not an island unto itself. It is deeply integrated with design, medium, theme, and the personality of the individual artist.

Artistic creativity—the combination of color and design—is not so much a choice of theme, but a choice of perception. When we express ourselves in art, we show the world how we perceive the subject matter. It is not surprising, then, that so many people can view and create art expressing the same theme so differently, as each of us has unique perceptions. Thus, creating is the process of observing and feeling the world around us, transposing those ideas into our own perceptions, and then translating these thoughts to the world as visual imageries.

The true artistry that lies within all of us is not academic, but intuitive. We must be patient with our growth, realizing that it is not a mere object that can be grasped instantaneously. Rather, creativity is a lifetime endeavor. If it is to remain viable within us, we must accept the reality that our creative ideas continually grow and develop.

May the information and ideas presented here give you support and incentive to make the choices that are best for your unique creative spirit. Whenever possible in this lifelong artistic journey, make the conscious decision to choose the paths less traveled . . . taking those that seem to call your name. As noted by one who has gone so gently before us . . . truly, it can make all the difference.

"All glory comes from daring to begin."
—Eugene Ware

"I began to see nature a little late. This does not, however, make it any less interesting.

—Paul Cézanne
French painter, 1839–1906
The Impressionists,
Portraits and Confidences

"I think that if one kind of property is sacred, it's the kind that is the product of our own minds, made with our own hands . . ."

—Camille Pissarro
French painter, 1830–1903
The Impressionists,
Portraits and Confidences

"Anything painted directly, on the spot, always has strength, a power, a lively touch that is lost in the studio. Your first impression is the right one. Stick to it and refuse to budge."

—Eugène Boudin
French painter, 1824–1898
The Impressionists,
Portraits and Confidences

"How I wish you were here! I should like to have your opinion about the choice of my landscape, and for my figures. Sometimes I'm afraid of going wrong."

—Claude Monet
French painter, 1840–1926
May 5, 1865, in a letter
to Frederic Bazille
The Impressionists,
Portraits and Confidences

CHAPTER 1

Colorful Beginnings

From the time we wake until we close our eyes at night, we are immersed in color. Yet we rarely think about color, nor do we consider how strongly it affects our lives. Quite simply, color pervades our physical world, affects our emotions, and gives others important clues about our personalities and moods. Thus, it is important to give color more than a passing glance in both our general living and in our creative endeavors.

In art, color is used as a visual language. It is the communication link between creator and viewer. Color is visually musical, being both rhythmic and lyrical. It sets the tempo of a design through the blending of a multitude of hues. Like beautiful melodies and poignant words, color draws from the deep emotions within us. It can be stunning or powerful; or color can evoke contemplation, serenity, or quiet comfort.

Whether we work intuitively or through a predetermined color plan, our personality is brought into the artwork by the way we interpret the design through the placement and use of color. Our color choices should elicit responses and images that are most appropriate for our personality and artistic purposes.

To begin developing individual color sense, learn as much as you can about your personal responses to color. Assess your color needs, dislikes, and loves. Be open enough to shed past beliefs that have no relevance to your life today. Be willing to open your eyes to new ideas and insights. Explore the diversity of color. Find the colors that reflect your personality, mood, and style most strongly.

When creating, give color and all its idiosyncrasies as much latitude as you would a child. Allow time and patience for your color sense to grow; allow color freedom of spirit, so that it may not feel too controlled; have courage to embrace it again, and again . . . even when it doesn't live up to your expectations or do as you had planned. Color is fluid and spontaneous; it does best under these conditions. If you allow yourself time to form a personal relationship with color, you will be able to create art that floats in your mind and sings in your soul.

It is both a challenge and a wonder to see visual images transformed into a surface design. With knowledge, guidelines, and ideas you can make your creative endeavors not only a reflection and an extension of yourself, but a reality.

FAMILIES OF COLORFUL PERSONALITIES

In ancient times, because colors vanished as darkness set in, people thought colors were given and taken away by the rulers of the mythical heavens, much as light was taken away. With this mystical association, colors were given divine importance. Some colors were even thought to have supernatural powers.

For centuries, historic symbols represented by different colors have evoked strong emotions within us. As in the past, color still plays a very important role in our daily lives, representing images, places, objects, ideas, and emotions. Our reactions can range from strongly emotional to nonexistent, or from positive to negative, depending on our life experiences, culture, and individual makeup.

Each color has its own beauty and individuality, which you may accept or reject. While reviewing the imageries and symbolisms of these color families, think about the colors that most affect you. Open your mind to using more colors than you are currently comfortable with by becoming more familiar with the color family hues. As you find yourself beginning to admire their unique qualities, you will incorporate more of these colors in your work. Eventually the entire color spectrum will become a part of your artistic expression, as it is in nature.

Restful Blues

The range of blue hues is vast, eliciting a broad array of images. The brilliant turquoise of a peacock differs from periwinkle blue flowers or the clear, cerulean blue of a midday sky. The blues of sapphires, blueberries, and hyacinths may relate somewhat to the night sky, but they are far different from the blues of rushing rivers or the sparkling ocean. Pristine mountain lakes often show yet another breathtaking blue, like their namesake, aquamarine. The grayed blues of distant hills and mountains are still another dimension of this diverse color family. These atmospheric blues are gray, yet they can also be tinged with lavender.

Figure 1-1 Blue Imagery: Midday Water and Sky

In the grand scheme of nature, blue is a major player in the background of our world, but is rarely exhibited in the living landscape. Therefore, we most often see blue as the color everything is set against. This results in blue becoming a striking contrast to the multitude of colors that make up the rest of the earth's beauty.

With the vastness of the blue sky as the backdrop for all other colors in our world, it seems natural that most of us are quite at ease with the color blue and its various offspring. In fact, it is likely that each of us is drawn to at least one of the hues within the blue family.

Many blues are brilliant and dazzling. Aquamarine lends itself to a happy, bubbly, warm mood. On the other hand, cooler blues often reflect feelings of airiness, peacefulness, serenity, and hope. In its grayed form, blue can be very atmospheric. Its darker hues can signify depth and mystery. Blue can be restful, refreshing, and certainly very cool. At the same time, blue can suggest sophistication, elegance, and formality.

Being surrounded by blue tends to decrease muscle activity, blood pressure, respiration, and heart rate. Blue, then, is an excellent color for bedrooms and other rooms meant for rest and respite.

Using Blue in Your Art

When choosing colors for your artwork, consider using the guidelines nature has set for herself—using blue as the serene backdrop. If you wish to create a quilt, or any artwork that gives the feeling of tranquillity, contemplate either using blue as your dominant color, or creating a work of art that uses only the blue family (photos 60, 62, 78, 79, 81).

Dark blue, like a midnight blue or ink navy, can be used like black to contrast bright, warm colors. When used in this way, the effect can be very dramatic and eye catching (photos 17, 18, 72). Used with its complement, orange, blue can help create the effect of simultaneous contrast (photo 25). Light blue can give an airy, fresh feeling (photo 32). Light, grayed blue, on the other hand, can

easily suggest a wintery scene or an icy mood (photos 50, 59, 79). A grayed blue-green, however, has too much warmth to appear icy (photo 30).

Luscious Green

Lush gardens, gently rolling meadows, tree-lined country roads, emeralds, dense forests, silky moss, swiftly moving mountain streams—all of these elicit images of green.

In its many varied hues, green is the color most often found in the landscape. Greens vary from the yellow greens of spent leaves to the bright grass greens of spring to the dark greens of the evergreens. Because of its dominant role in the landscape, green is most often set against the blue sky. For this reason, blue and green are well recognized as one of the most beautiful color combinations with which to surround ourselves.

Symbolically, green is closely associated with nature. For centuries the natural concepts of birth, rebirth, life, growth, healing, rest, and regeneration have been linked with green. It also represents, somewhat incongruously, both a plentiful bounty and an unripened or immature harvest. Green reflects the freshness and joy of youth.

Green—A Soothing Source

Green is created by blending the two primary colors yellow and blue (turquoise). In its own way, green acts as a neutral color because it lies between both warm and cool hues on the color wheel. Green tends to give balance to the temperature of the two colors, resulting in a calming visual effect. As a color, it is much more passive than active in its feeling. People are more contemplative when surrounded with green. Since our eyes can focus easily on the color green, it tends to relax the eye. Therefore, with respect to most of the hues within the family, green is an easy color to be around.

Using Green in Art

Green reacts to other colors in a design as it does in nature. It is a lovely contrast and companion to yellows, pinks, roses, peaches, apricots, purples, and blues (photos 22, 29, 30, 37, 40). It is so plentiful in nature and can

Figure 1-2 Green Imagery: Green Grass

give such an uplifting feeling that with thoughtful care green can work well with almost any other color. Naturally, it works beautifully with the intermingled colors of its complement magenta (red) and afterimage pink (photos 68, 80).

Whenever green is added to a warm color, it immediately acts as a coolant (photo 30). When it reacts as a cool color, such as mint green, it will recede within the design. However, yellow greens and forest greens are usually considered warm and tend to advance in a design (photos 22, 29, 40). Green has the ability to neutralize the visual power of red and magenta, primarily because of its close complementary association (photo 70).

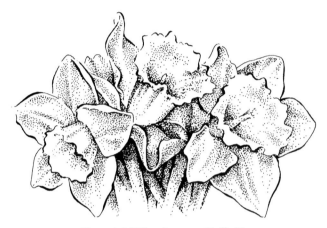

Figure 1-3 Yellow Imagery: Daffodils

Joyful Yellow

Nothing seems so brilliant and warm as a beautiful day glowing with sunshine. Yellow makes us think of such things as lemonade, butterflies, and corn on the cob. Those of us living in cool climates may dream of California, Florida, Italy, Greece, or Spain . . . lands warmed by golden sun. The delicate Peace rose, yellow with a touch of pink, and the flawless pale yellow of the Irish Gold rose remind us of the exquisiteness of nature. The yellow hues of harvest grains are more mellow. The deeper yellows of gold bring us images of coins, jewelry, and metals.

Historically, yellow has played an important part in many cultures. Ancient legend depicted gold as the son of the sun. For China, yellow is the imperial color. Gold, part of the yellow family, is the most desired metal in the world, and has been sought after for centuries. Throughout the world, yellow is a color that brings joy to people as it lifts their spirits. It is the color of laughter and happiness.

No matter where we live, after a dreary winter we are all excited to see the first signs of spring: yellow primroses, crocuses, daffodils, and tulips. Summer brings us a host of yellow flowers, from the traditional children's favorite, the dandelion, to buttercups, daisies, and dahlias.

Yellow is the lightest and brightest color in the color wheel. When properly placed, yellow can glow with unbelievable luminosity. Its spirited personality adds a cheerful quality to any work of art. Also, because of its brilliance, it can advance to the surface of a design (photos 17, 19, 21, 23, 24).

When using yellow in your artwork, be aware of its visual strength. Since the eye automatically focuses on yellow, it can take over a design with very little difficulty, perhaps even bringing focus to an unwanted element. Yellow is a wonderful accent, but a little bit of yellow can go a long way.

As yellow mixes with other colors, it begins to lose its identity. When you mix even a miniscule amount of green with yellow, it immediately takes on a green hue. When a small amount of magenta or red is added to yellow, it becomes orange. No other color is as sensitive to another hue as is yellow. As soon as yellow is darkened with black or toned with gray or violet, its brightness and clarity are lost. It immediately loses its personality and spirited appeal. Blackened yellow begins to look like a muddy olive. Toned yellow turns to tans and beiges (photos 26, 27, 28, 30).

Delectable Orange

The orange family brings thoughts of food to our attention. Juicy oranges, succulent cantaloupes, tree-ripened peaches, apricots sweet with aroma, and the tropical fruits papaya and mango come to mind. Winter dinner tables are brightened with squash, carrots, sweet potatoes, and pumpkin pies. With this splendid array of food, it is not surprising that the orange family is noted for stimulating appetites.

Examples of orange hues are also abundant in the flower garden. Rose gardeners delight in the blossoms from fluorescent orange Tropicana and coral-orange Montezuma. For those shady areas, lovely orange hues of impatiens bloom profusely, ranging from light apricot to dark coral. Nearby, coral begonias happily burst forth. Dahlias range in color from golden oranges to warm

Figure 1-4 Orange Imagery: Fruit

rusts. The flowers from this color family are as visually sumptuous as a platter of fresh fruit of the same hues.

Orange's many hues provide us with a warm earthiness. The cool nights of autumn cause turning colors on broad-leaved trees. These glorious annual shows of nature come together with breathtaking wonder, combining such colors as copper, orange, rust, russet, and brown. Far from these autumnal events, deserts elsewhere in the world silently glisten with sand of orange, rust, tan, golden brown, and copper.

Dawn is presented primarily by the yellow and orange family—soft creams, yellows, apricots, and peaches. Later, the evening sunset can be intensified by the deep, vibrant oranges. Summer nights may find us happily singing around a campfire, roasting marshmallows on the glowing orange embers. The orange family brings us varied options in its many hues, ranging from delicate flowers and gentle summer sunrises to the earthiness of fall and intense winter sunsets.

Figure 1-5 Red Imagery: Red Tulips

USING ORANGE IN ART

Orange is a blend of red and yellow. As would be expected from the offspring of such a pair, orange has many characteristics of both parent colors. Like yellow, orange is filled with energy and warmth. The more yellow in the orange, the more glowing it becomes. The closer it gets to red, the more heated orange becomes, giving a stronger emotional appeal. Orange can suggest flamboyance, especially when a mixture of oranges is used within an artwork. Examples of quilts using the orange family are photos 16, 17, 23, 25, 30, and 72.

Like yellow, too much pure orange can be uncomfortable for the eyes. It is best as either an accent or blended with other hues to dilute its strength. Research has determined that surrounding ourselves with orange tends to stimulate creativity and hunger. Too much orange can be detrimental, causing discomfort and nervousness.

Vivacious Red

Reds are a varied group; orange-reds, pure red, brownish reds, magenta, and purplish reds are major members of this family. The gentlest color is pink. Its soft, quiet, feminine nature does not elicit any of the strong emotions that are noted among the related hues. Examples of quilts using hues from the red color family are photos 16, 17, 19, 20, 43, 70, and 72.

There are many examples of red in nature. The blazing strength of red is most often shown in garden splendor. Two favorite rhododendrons, Elizabeth and Jean Marie De Montague, are welcome accents to springtime greenery in temperate climates. Rose lovers find an abundance of their favorite flowers in the red hues. Oklahoma, one of the blackest reds, is a strong contrast

to the stately Mister Lincoln, a rich red, or Christian Dior, a lovely cherry red.

Poppies, zinnias, and geraniums show wonderful splotches of bright red against green shrubs and blue sky in summer. The crab apple, flowering plum, Japanese maple, pink flowering dogwood, and red flowering gum tree are all fine examples of red in nature. Of course, in autumn, when the leaves turn color, some change to many hues of red. Sumac trees and smoke bushes are glorious with their magnificent red leaves, seeming almost unreal in their brilliance.

The delicate pinks, the softest hue in the red family, are an important part of the spring reawakening each year. Kwansan flowering cherry trees are one of many varieties that line streets throughout the world in wondrous splendor. Azaleas and rhododendrons bloom profusely, with hundreds of different pink hybrids to awe the viewer.

Cleverly, nature balances the reds of the landscape with enticements of another kind—sweet, tart, hot, and unusual food. The diverse colorations of food alone provide countless studies of how complex the red family is and how the hues interact with each other. A platter piled high with fruits and vegetables gives ample visual stimulation to inspire many artworks using the emotive reds.

Red onions, tomatoes, red leafy lettuce, and red cabbages give a beautiful contrast to the other green and yellow vegetables we eat. Tart rhubarb with its pinky red coloring combines beautifully with sweet orange-red strawberries. A summer picnic wouldn't be complete without watermelon or juicy red cherries. The plum family is beautiful with its varied colors and flavors. Berries also provide a wonderful sampling of the hues within the red family. Huckleberries and raspberries mix beautifully with black-tinged boysenberries, loganberries, and blackberries.

Nature also provides us with some wonderful nonedible examples of red, such as the dark red garnet and the deep red translucent ruby. Bricks are made from reddened earth. Some bricks move closer to the orange hues, while others are almost brownish purple. Of course, the intense red hues of strong sunsets are always excellent to study. The red cardinal is a fine example of strong red coloring in the animal world.

The Physical Aspects of Red

Red is powerful. It is the most emotional color we can see. Red elicits excitement, intensity, and fervor. Anger, aggression, passion, love, bravery, blood, strength, life, and fire are all tightly bound to the emotional, mental, and physical images of the red color family. Like yellow, even the smallest amount of pure red catches our immediate attention. Red is very reflective and can have a great luminous effect.

Physically, red is the strongest and longest ray of all the colors in a light wave; thus it affects the eye's retina more than any other color. It also automatically sets up a physical reaction in many people. Red can raise our blood pressure, quicken our pulse, and increase our breathing rate. Red also increases muscle activity. Being surrounded by red usually stimulates the brain. This in turn sets up the adrenal glands to pump adrenalin into the body, causing a temporary spurt of energy. If we remain surrounded by red for a long time, fatigue can set in, because most of us cannot withstand the continual physical changes that take place in our bodies when constantly stimulated.

Using Red in Art

Red, like yellow, can be an attention grabber in an artwork. It can easily stimulate or excite the viewer. Because it draws the eye so easily, the most brilliant reds should be the dominant feature or focal point in the artwork. If you only want small smatterings of red in your art as an accent, limit the amount of red, being careful to place the accents in the design so they do not detract from the focus. Diluting the color by making it a shade, tone, or tint can allow you to include more red in a picture where it needs to play a secondary role.

Purple—The Queen of Color

Purple, a very rich hue, is a blend of various forms of blue and red (magenta). This family of colors includes purple, violet, lavender, mauve, blue-violet, and red-violet. Purple is quite rare in nature. Exceptions include the night sky and flowers such as pansies, violets, and irises.

Being an offspring of blue and red, purple tends to carry the traits of both hues. Love, courage, spirit, and wisdom are felt subconsciously in the presence of the color purple. It also can be a color of long-enduring sadness or long-past mourning. Mostly, however, it is a color of regality and grandness.

Purple was a latecomer to the color world and was extremely difficult to obtain centuries ago. Consequently, it became the favorite color of ancient rulers. Throughout the ages it has been the color for nobility. Even to this day, purple is used by royalty during special ceremonies.

Blue-violet is considered a cool color, suggesting individuality and solitude. Red-violet, a warmer color, gives off a more luminous feeling than its cooler partner. Red-violet evokes both strength and splendor, and is sometimes used in religious attire and ceremonies.

Using Purple in Art

Colors from the purple family elicit a wide variety of emotional responses, so its use in art can vary according to artistic goals. The purple hues give the artist many choices, from lavender and mauve to plum and eggplant. Even the blued periwinkle colors can easily intermingle with the purple family. You can be quite bold, using the strongest of the purple family, or you can create a delicate, soft visual effect. You have countless choices in selecting the most appropriate hue.

If you use the dark, shadowy colors of purple, bring life to the art by working with its complement or afterimage. For most art, it is important to balance purple's heaviness with other color choices. Certainly, the theme and overall design will be the key to how you create art using the purple family effectively. Examples of artwork using the purple family includes photos 40, 43, 50, 52, 54–56, 73–76, and 84–86.

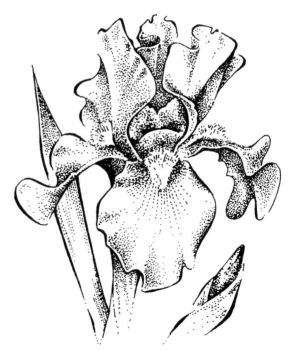

Figure 1-6 Purple Imagery: Purple Iris

CHAPTER 2

Using Color Naturally

Colors surround us in nature, constantly changing, blending, and flowing into both subtle and vibrant designs. Nature is so perfect in her use of color that we often take her nuances for granted, thus ignoring some of the most wonderful color lessons. Man has never been able to improve the color system developed and refined by nature, although he has often tried.

We have known since childhood that nature segregates colors by season. Each season of the year has its own color characteristics and emotional responses. In addition, nature also categorizes by daily cycle, from sunrise to nightfall, and then back to sunrise again.

Each year we watch the cycle of nature bring its colorations and moods to us. Every spring, greenery emerges from the brown, gray ground of winter. New plants bud and early spring flowers burst forth. The fragile freshness of spring is, of course, the lead-in for amazing splashes of summer color, with its brilliant green grasses, flourishing plants and trees, and the magnificent colors of flowers, birds, and insects.

After the wonder of summer, with its colors at their most intense level, comes autumn—bringing us the last hurrah of color before the annual cycle comes to a close. Although autumn colors are gorgeous, their brilliance has little relation to the vivid colors of the season before. Their autumnal mood reflects change, preparing us for the last phase in the cycle of nature and color.

The yearly cycle of both life and color closes with a hush. In peaceful repose, the bareness of winter lies nestled in subdued, gray colors. This dormancy is a welcome pause from the stimulation of the previous seasons. Each year these seasonal cycles blend one into another with harmony, beauty, color, and elegant grace.

For the most part, the daily color cycle imitates the seasonal color system. Sunrise begins with gentle colors, bringing hope to a new day, much like the soft, quiet rebirth of spring. As the sun rises, the brilliant sunlight shines vividly on the earth, displaying life in its brightest clarity. It is the time of day most like summer. As dusk moves in, evening colors come forth to close the day. Soon darkness brings the night colors. Then as morning begins to break again, the grayed tones emerge from the darkness, closing the cycle and setting the stage for the rebirth of another day.

These two cycles are predictable and inevitable, always working together, yet separate in their purposes. Each elicits distinct moods and colorations. With a little thought we can put these seasonal and daily color patterns into use, creating art that not only speaks from our intuitive soul, but emits emotional responses that reveal our mood of the moment. These two cycles can also provide us with a solid foundation for using color most effectively.

THE FOUR COLOR SCALES

Color scales play a role similar to the function of musical scales. They give fundamental order to the various elements of color. Color scales are broken into four major divisions: pure hues, tints, shades, and tones. Within each scale there can be a countless series of ascending and descending colors. The specific interval between hues within a scale can vary depending on the artist's needs. These scales are easy to understand because we've lived with them our entire lives.

The four natural color scales, in seasonal order, are tints, pure hues, shades, and tones. For ease in learning, however, they will be presented in a slightly different order, the pure hues being introduced first. As mentioned previously, each scale has its own personality and requirements. Each scale also plays an integral part in setting the mood or theme in a work of art. (See photos 2 and 4 for an example of all four scales represented in one color family.)

Most of us prefer one scale over another. Often we use this scale without even being aware we are doing so. This happens because we have subconsciously processed

Figure 2-1 Pure Color Scale: Summer Imagery

nature's color scales in our minds, and we are in tune with both nature and our inner voice.

Contrastingly, there will probably be one color scale each of us avoids as much as possible. Its use as a dominant scale is more than we can handle visually. However, when we work with these colors in the manner nature has chosen, we find that all the scales can be pleasing. Certainly there are times when each plays an important role in our artistic desires.

The Pure Color Scale

Primary colors and all colors created by blending primary colors are pure colors. Pure colors are the most vibrant. Often these are the intense colors in sunsets, blooming flowers, tropical fish, and wild birds. These pure colors are the hues of summer. They are defined as pure because they have no white, black, or gray in them to distort their vibrant clarity. Even though this scale of colors is the least represented in nature, when these hues are present they dazzle us with their brilliance (figure 2-1, photo 1).

Art made from this color scale can be quite dynamic. These colors draw our eyes immediately. They demand attention, and generally get it. Not only are works of art from the pure scale visually strong, but they can also be emotionally powerful. To create art high in visual impact or filled with kinetic energy, pure hues should dominate the work (photos 19–21, 23). If you want to create art that is quite summery in its emotional appeal or theme, again, choose your colors from this scale.

The pure colors most commonly used are yellow, yellow-green, green, blue-green, turquoise, blue, violet, purple, magenta, red, orange, and yellow-orange.

Most people are rather apprehensive about using pure colors in large amounts. For their personal comfort, these hues can be overwhelming. If you are uncomfortable with the strength of pure hues, simply use small amounts of these colors as accents to add vibrance. You may find that the more you work with pure hues, the more you enjoy including them in your art.

People who have gregarious, extroverted personalities usually feel quite at home using strong, intense colors from the pure scale. They enjoy the energy and happy feeling these colors emit. These strong colors visually convey their personal spirit and energetic style. People who love to work in pure colors often find most other color scales difficult to work with because they lack the desired drama and excitement. For them, bold colors from the pure scale bring life to their works of art.

If you wish to use a neutral with pure colors, black accentuates the dramatic effect best. Grays work quite well in certain situations. White may be the least desirable of all

Figure 2-2 Tint Color Scale: Spring Imagery

neutrals to use, unless of course you want to create art with highly contrasting values.

Pure hues have a role in attaining certain illusions. When you are striving for iridescence, the best results are achieved with splashes of pure colors amidst the dark shades. Other illusions, like luminosity and luster, can be created with bits of pure hues intermingled with hues from other color scales. Pure colors are also used when creating highlights.

Pure Scale Mentors

Art that predominantly uses the pure scale seems especially free in spirit. Often it dances with vibrance. Even if you yourself are not especially comfortable using pure hues as your dominant visual scale, take time to enjoy the works of many of our most famous artists who loved working with energetic colors. Scores of art books show examples of boldly colorful artworks by such great artists as Henri Matisse, Paul Gauguin, Stuart Davis, Pablo Picasso, Vincent Van Gogh, and Georgia O'Keeffe.

Many quilt artists are known for their strong use of color. Nancy Crow, Yvonne Porcella, and Caryl Fallert are widely known for their dramatic color use.

The Tint Scale

The dramatic mood of pure colors is counterbalanced by the delicate nature of tints. Tints are colors which have had white added to them. If a small amount of white is added to the pure color, the new color will be similar to the pure hue, but just a bit lighter than the original color. The lightest tint is a blush—white with just a tinge of a color added to it. Most tints are somewhere between these two extremes (photo 2A).

The colors in the tint scale reflect spring. They convey a gentle, soft mood. Tints are also sunrise colors—the fresh, hopeful hues of a new day. If you wish to represent images of spring or an early morning, either in color or design, the majority of your colors should come from the tint scale (figure 2-2).

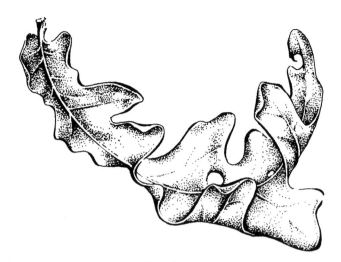

Figure 2-3 Shade Scale: Autumn Imagery

The most commonly recognized hues in the tint scale are the soft, delicate pastels. Lavender, pink, apricot, peach, powder blue, mint green, robin's-egg blue, and cream are some of our most commonly recognized tints.

Interestingly, white added to a color acts as a coolant. So tints tend to appear cool. Tints are also light and airy. The most natural neutral to use with the tint scale is white, because all tints are created with white. If you use an off-white (grayed or yellowed) with tints, it may deaden the artwork, destroying the freshness you are trying to attain.

The delicate colors in the tint scale can be used in many illusions. Tints are widely used to attain opalescence, luminosity, and luster.

THE TINT SCALE MENTORS

When we think of renowned paintings done in the tint scale, we immediately picture works of many French Impressionists. Claude Monet is probably the most famous Impressionist who often painted in the tint scale. Monet's paintings are light, airy, and uplifting. In the quilt world, the tint scale has not been widely used to this date. For examples of work in the tint scale, see photos 25, 30–32, and 43.

The Shade Scale

Pure colors mixed with black become shades. With a small amount of black added, the color is only slightly darker than the pure hue; the more black added, the darker the color becomes. Some shades, like ink navy and eggplant, can seem almost black. Shades are always darker than the pure color. The most natural neutral to use with shades is black, because it is present in all shades (photo 2B).

Shades have two distinct personalities, depending on whether the colors are visually warm or cool. Both warm and cool shades are very useful when you want to

incorporate luminosity, luster, and shadows in your artwork. Cool shades are also needed to create iridescence.

THE WARM SHADES

Warm hues from the shade scale are strongly autumnal. These fall colors are rich, deep, and earthy. Browns, golds, rusts, coppers, burnt oranges, olives, and pumpkins are all part of this wonderful fall color scheme. If you want to create art that reflects autumn, it must be done with this color scale (figure 2-3; photos 16, 17, 26, 29).

BROWN AND RUST

Two warm shades, brown and rust, can be difficult to work with because they are derivatives of several different pure hues. As black is added to different oranges and reds, the color changes to several shades of rust. As black is increased, the colors become brown. Generally, if you are working with reds and want to include a brown or rust in your picture, use one that has red in its root color. If you are working with oranges, the brown to use would have an orange base. Likewise, the rust would be in the same orange range.

You can purposely choose a brown or rust that clashes with the other colors in your art to add interest or attention. If this is your intent, and it is done with care, you can achieve great results. When it happens unplanned, it can be extremely disappointing to use a brown that is visually distracting because it comes from the wrong root color. The artistic effect can be destroyed. Therefore, know what visual outcome you desire and select the appropriate brown or rust color.

THE COOL NIGHT SHADES

The cool hues of the shade scale are quite different from the warm hues. Naturally, you use cool hues to create evening and night scenes. Also, if you want a mystical feeling or a sense of great depth, the cool colors are perfect. Deep water scenes may also use the beautiful blues, greens, and violets of this scale. Maroon, plum, navy,

Figure 2-4 Shade Scale: Night Imagery

forest green, and ultramarine blue are also hues from this shade color scale (figure 2-4; photos 69, 72, 77, 81).

Over the ages, many powerful artists have used the shade scale to create magnificent pictures. Leonardo da Vinci, Rembrandt, Velazquez, Rousseau, Delacroix, Cezanne, and America's James McNeill Whistler are a handful of those whose talents have given the world a stunning array of artwork to enjoy.

Many quilt artists bring the rich hues of the shade scale together to create art of unsurpassed beauty. Erika Odemer, Mary Morgan, and Suzanne Kjelland have all created stunning quilts from the shade scale.

The Tone Scale

The remaining group of colors belongs to the tone scale. Tones are created by graying a pure color. Depending on the value of the gray, a tone can be lighter than the pure color, the same value, or darker than the pure color. When we talk about a color being toned down, we imply that it has been grayed. Since gray appears in all tones, it is the most appropriate neutral when creating artwork with these hues.

Tones can project a misty or wintery effect. They are the perfect scale for all winter scenes (figure 2-5). Some of our most common tones include beige, rose, slate blue, sage green, and heather. Examples using the tone scale include photos 2C, 27, 28, 35, 36, and 48–58.

Use tones when you wish to create illusions of depth (photos 50, 58), luminosity (photos 9, 44, 47, 73, 85), and opalescence (photos 30, 49, 51). In some circumstances, tones can create a lustrous effect (photos 48, 60). Shadows may also be attained through the use of tones.

THE TONE SCALE MENTORS

When thinking of artwork in the tone scale, the greatest group of artists who come to mind, again, are the French Impressionists. The majority of their work was created in the high-valued colors in the tint and tone scales. Monet, Manet, Degas, Renoir, and Pissarro were as impressive with their beautifully toned paintings as they were when using other scales. In the quilt world, many talented artists work in the tone scale. Nancy Halpern, Janice Richards, Judy Dales, Miriam Nathan-Roberts, and Pat Magaret are very much at home with these soft, subdued colors (photos 35, 36, 48, 49, 53, 60).

USING COLOR EXPRESSIVELY

Even though you may prefer a particular color scale, you will probably work with all the scales during your creative endeavors. Some scales may be used primarily as accents; others may be needed to attain certain illusions.

Figure 2-5 Tone Scale: Winter Imagery

If you work in a harmonious fashion, as nature does, you will probably enjoy working with all the scales, using them as your needs and emotions change. Several quilt and textile artists frequently create beautiful works of art using different dominant scales. Michael James, Caryl Fallert, Alison Goss, Amanda Richardson, Karen Perrine, and Carol Ann Wadley are noted for their versatility in color use.

If you strongly dislike certain colors or combinations of colors, it may be because the colors have been taken out of nature's context. These negative reactions are often provoked by subconscious memories from our past or by the way colors have been manipulated in our home and work environment. Rarely do we obtain these intense dislikes from nature's display; therefore, if we become more in tune with the way color works in nature, we may be able to release our negative reactions to certain colors.

Try to imitate both the visual beauty and the emotional appeal of nature's colors whenever possible. Learn through nature how to use color so that it makes your soul sing and reflects your mood. Begin by making small, simple observations. Perhaps you'll study a sunset and watch how the colors interact and change from minute to minute. Maybe you're more interested in observing the color strata of flowers in a rose garden. Once you begin exploring color regularly, your comfort level will grow. Thus your ability to incorporate more colors within your artwork will increase. Give yourself a realistic time span in which to expand your ideas and knowledge about color, and enjoy the challenges and steps along the way.

"Art is harmony parallel to nature."
—Paul Cézanne
French painter, 1839–1906
The Impressionists,
Portraits and Confidences

CHAPTER 3

Colorful Intrigues

Putting colors together in art can be both exciting and frustrating. It can bring great results . . . and sometimes curious surprises. Choosing colors is an evolving process. Depending on your desires, you will select colors differently each time you set out on a new artistic adventure.

When creating, consider the colors and their nuances within a design as ingredients. Major ingredients carry the theme throughout the entire design, while minor ones add spice and zest to give the art interest and appeal. It is especially intriguing to explore the myriad possibilities and combinations when ingredients are added, substituted, rearranged, or refocused.

Using nature's clues allows you the opportunity to express yourself in many more ways than you might originally have thought possible. Additionally, with basics in hand, you have the freedom to create in your own style, while being reasonably assured of knowing what direction your art will take. Some of nature's most basic and popular effects are introduced in this chapter. Guidelines and practical information are included as well as historic background information.

LIGHT AND COLOR

Much of our current knowledge about color and light developed from Sir Isaac Newton's innovative experiments during the seventeenth century. Through Newton's studies we learned that without light there is no color. As darkness descends, color diminishes. When we are enveloped in darkness, we see no color.

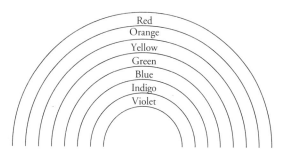

Figure 3-1 The Rainbow Spectral Colors
The rainbow colors are always located in the same order, starting with red on the outside and ending with violet on the innermost curve.

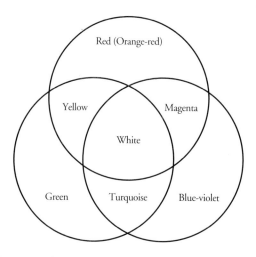

Figure 3-2 The Additive Color Circles: The Colors of Light
The additive (light) primaries are red (an orange-red), green, and blue-violet. When mixed, red and green become yellow; green and blue-violet become turquoise; and blue-violet and red become magenta. When the three light primaries are combined, white light is seen because all color is reflected.

The rainbow intrigued Sir Isaac Newton. He found he could duplicate rainbow colors by bending light rays through a glass prism. His investigations proved that light waves could be broken into individual colors when they were bent.

When light waves strike objects such as raindrops or prisms, the colors separate, exhibiting a beautiful array of colors: red, orange, yellow, green, blue, indigo, and violet. These colors are called *spectral colors* because they span the entire spectrum of both the rainbow and a light wave. The colors are always located in the same order in the spectrum (figure 3-1).

Newton found that red, the longest wavelength and the most gradual curve in the spectrum, is always on the outside of the rainbow's arc. It also has the slowest vibration rate of all the colors. Red promotes a feeling of warmth or heat. In contrast, violet, which is always found on the inside of the rainbow's arc, has the shortest wavelength, thus curving the most, and its wavelength has the fastest vibration rate. Violets and blues suggest coolness.

Sir Isaac Newton was the first person to organize colors in a circular pattern. His color wheel was formed by placing the seven colors of the rainbow around a circle.

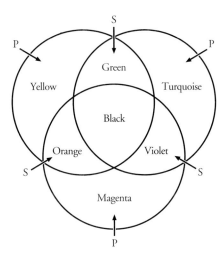

Figure 3-3 The Subtractive Primary Colors:
The Colors of Pigments and Dyes
The subtractive primaries are yellow, magenta, and turquoise.
Mixing the three primaries together results in black because
all color is absorbed.

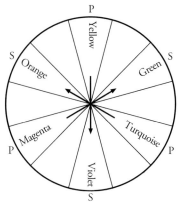

Figure 3-4 Subtractive Primary Colors and Their Complements
The secondary colors of green, violet, and orange are formed by
mixing, respectively, the primaries yellow and turquoise; turquoise
and magenta; and magenta and yellow. Each secondary color sits
opposite the primary color from which it has no parentage and
is its complement.

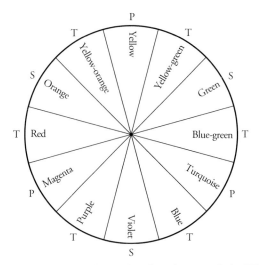

Figure 3-5 The Ives Color Circle: The Subtractive Color Wheel
12-step color wheel includes three primary colors,
three secondary colors, and six tertiary (intermediate) colors.

Since his organization of colors in 1666, artists, physicists, psychologists, and others have established their own color wheels. Each color wheel differs slightly in the colors it includes and in its primary colors. They all illustrate important color relationships within particular disciplines. Some fields, like art, may use more than one color wheel.

Colored Light and the Additive Color Wheel

Although it may not play a significant role in our art, we should be aware that colors in light function differently from pigments and dyes. When colored light is mixed, the colors of each combine together to form a new hue. This new color ends up being more brilliant than either of the parent colors due to the combination of all the properties added to it. This process of adding light colors together is called *additive color mixing*.

Primary colors are hues that all other colors are made from. In the light color wheel, primary colors are red (an orange-red), green, and blue-violet (figure 3-2). When red and green combine together, they become yellow. When green and blue-violet mix together, their total creates turquoise. Blue-violet and red will become magenta. These three new hues are called *secondary colors*.

When all three primary colors are added together, they reflect back to us as a complete light wave, thus forming white light (figure 3-2).

PIGMENTS AND DYES

Pigments and dyes combine through subtractive color mixing. When two different paints are mixed together on paper, the color characteristics that are identical in both hues are absorbed into the surface, becoming invisible. The remaining elements, or leftover hues, combine to form a new color. When we see only the colors that are a result of this subtraction process, it is called *subtractive color mixing*.

The Subtractive Color Wheel

The color wheel most appropriate for our own field of pigments and dyes is the Ives Color Circle. In this color wheel, the primary colors, or those hues that all colors are created from, are yellow, magenta, and turquoise (figure 3-3). Blending these colors gives beautiful, clear, vivid colors (photo 1). Notice that the three primary colors of this color wheel are the secondary colors of the additive color wheel.

In the Ives Color Wheel, mixing the primary colors yellow and turquoise results in green; the combination of turquoise and magenta is violet; and the blending of magenta and yellow is orange. These are called secondary colors. As you can see by figure 3-4, each secondary color sits opposite the primary color from which it has no parentage.

If you further blend the primary colors together to form a twelve-step color wheel, six new colors will be created: yellow-green, blue-green, blue, purple, red, and yellow-orange (figure 3-5). These colors that lie between the secondary and primary colors are called tertiary colors or intermediate colors. You can continue to combine colors, forming a twenty-four-step color wheel, a forty-eight-step color wheel, or one with as many hues as you like (photo 1).

Mixing the three paint primaries together creates a blackish color. Because all the color elements are duplicated when the primaries are combined, no color can be reflected back, as there are no leftover colors (figure 3-3).

COLOR TEMPERATURE

Colors can suggest feelings of warmth or coolness. This temperature leaning can subconsciously affect our mood. Warm colors are associated with sunlight, heat, and happiness. They have more ability to be luminous than cool colors do. Cool colors are associated with night, shadows, and mystery, and to some degree can evoke a feeling of heaviness. Warm colors advance visually, while cool colors tend to recede.

Although yellows, oranges, and reds are considered warm colors while greens, blues, and violets are considered cool, in reality all colors can be perceived as either cool or warm. Blue can appear warm if yellow is added to it. Likewise, green can appear warm or cool, depending on whether there is more yellow or blue in the mixture. Realizing that colors can vary in their suggestive temperature can help you make some decisions about how to interpret your design and how to use color to its best advantage in your art.

Colors are fluid and ever-changing in their effect, depending on their placement and the surrounding colors. If you want warm hues in your art to appear even warmer than they are, place them next to obviously cool colors. This will accentuate their warmth (photo 17). In contrast, some warm colors recede into the background when they are surrounded by even warmer hues. Setting a slightly blued red next to an orange-red causes the former to recede even though it is from the red family (photos 16, 42, 43).

If you want to accentuate cool colors, place them next to warm colors. A teal appears cooler next to warm yellow; the same teal appears warmer next to blue-violet (photo 14A). Although tints are considered cool, they often advance when placed around colors that appear cooler than they do.

Black is more closely associated with warmth than with coolness. Perhaps black is often considered warm because it absorbs heat. White is usually considered a cool color. It reflects heat, causing it to hint of coolness. White is also associated with snow, ice, and frost. To make almost any color appear cooler, add white, blue, or a blue-violet to the color.

A PARTNERSHIP: VALUE AND COLOR

Most of us react to art simply from its darkness or lightness rather than its subject matter. We are so sensitive to light that it affects our personality, our emotions, and even our physical activity. Therefore, choosing how light or dark an artwork will be is every bit as important as choosing colors.

In the art world, the word *value* is used to describe the lightness or darkness of a color. Colors close to white are called high in value; colors that are near black are low in value. Those hues that are close to neither black nor white are middle-valued colors. See photo 3 for examples. The value of a color often is related to the color scale used. The relative value of art is often described as a key. Art may be high keyed (light), middle keyed (middle valued), or low keyed (dark).

The most dominant color value in your art will determine the mood you create, either subtly or dramatically. Because value affects the outcome of the art in statement, design, and focus, many artists decide the value they will work with before choosing colors. Remember that colors appear to change their values as they relate to other colors. This illusion seems extraordinary when we watch color values appear to shift in a design. The narrow strip of middle green and gray in photo 3 illustrates how colors appear to change as they move from one value to another. Examples of using contrasting values include photos 43, 56, 61, 62, 67, 69, 86.

Pure Colors and Value

The pure color highest in value is yellow because it is the lightest color in the color wheel and the hue closest to white. In contrast, the pure color lowest in value is violet, because it is the darkest color on the color wheel and the one nearest to black (photo 1). Blue-green and orange-red are considered middle-valued colors in their pure form because they are about halfway between white and black in their value (figure 3-6).

High Values—High Key

High-keyed art is created in tints and high-valued tones. It is often light, soft, and airy. Generally, a high-key color scheme elicits a cheerful mood. Often high-key work is considered feminine. If you want to create a beautiful work of art that promotes a feeling of delicacy,

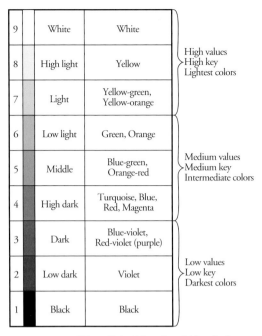

9	White	White	
8	High light	Yellow	High values, High key, Lightest colors
7	Light	Yellow-green, Yellow-orange	
6	Low light	Green, Orange	
5	Middle	Blue-green, Orange-red	Medium values, Medium key, Intermediate colors
4	High dark	Turquoise, Blue, Red, Magenta	
3	Dark	Blue-violet, Red-violet (purple)	
2	Low dark	Violet	Low values, Low key, Darkest colors
1	Black	Black	

Figure 3-6 Pure Color Nine-Step Value Scale

using tints and high-valued tones is an excellent start (photos 2A, 2C, 3).

If you want to create art in high key or high value, be certain you have some value contrasts in your design. Value changes in high-keyed art are done in small steps with gentle contrasts (photos 25, 26, 30, 32, 35). You may even want to create some accents with middle-valued colors (photo 73). If all the hues come from the same value scale, the design elements often blend into one another, becoming difficult to see.

Middle Values—Medium Key

Middle-valued or middle-keyed art is neither close to white nor black. Rather, it is somewhere in between those two colors (photos 3, 37). If you are more comfortable creating with the middle-valued colors, be certain to include value changes within this key. For contrast, you may have a few colors in high key or some in low key. If you use only middle-value colors, your design elements may disappear, resulting in uninteresting art.

Low Values—Low Key

Low-keyed art is quite dark, leaning toward black. It suggests an emotional feeling of strength, richness, and masculinity (photos 2B, 3, 16, 64, 70, 72, 77). If you work in the low values, be particularly aware that having no value changes can make your picture dull and lifeless. If there is too much black or darkness, the effect you are trying to create can become lost. It is best to add a value change in an accent to give some contrast. However, do not make the contrast so strong that it will distract rather than enhance.

Values and Past Artists

Claude Monet is one of the most famous artists who used the high-value scale. He worked mainly with tints and tones. His artwork is considered uplifting, gentle, and delicate. Some artists never include black in their artwork. One such group was the French Impressionists. The exception was Renoir, who loved black. He called black the "queen of colors." Throughout the ages, he has been one of the most successful artists to use black. James McNeill Whistler and Rembrandt are also renowned for their success in working predominantly with low values. These great painters were able to use black and deep shades to create the exact images they desired.

CREATING IN A VALUE KEY

Each of us tends to lean toward one key or another when working in art. When you think about beginning a project, visualize it. The key that you see in your mind will be the most successful one for you to work in. You have a natural affinity with values and colors that you can visualize. Even when you find yourself influenced by other opinions, pictures, or ideas, stay with your visualization.

You can change the key of your art if the values of the proposed design or inspiration are different than you visualize, or if they do not relate to a particular mood you wish to promote in your art. Thus, a low-valued design can be created in high key, if you so choose.

Transposing the value key in art is similar to the way a musician transposes music from one key to another. In both art and music, changing the key affects the mood and expression of the art. If you are inspired by a setting, but the setting's key is wrong for the mood you wish to evoke, feel free to transpose the values into a different key. Making a somber low-valued design into a light, airy high-key work can be done quite well simply by changing the values of the colors.

When you create a work of art, determine your focus. Then decide which key best suits your needs. Make this your dominant key. A dominant key in your artwork will automatically create unity. No unity can be attained when value keys are equally distributed. However, remember that not all colors have to be from one particular key.

INTENSITY

An intense color is fully colored in its purest form. It has not been diluted by any other color. A color is diluted when white, black, gray, or any other hue is added. In the context of this book, a color is considered less intense when it has been visually grayed. Technically, graying can occur from simply adding gray (or a black-and-white combination); from adding the color's complement or afterimage; or from adding a small amount of the color's two closest adjacent colors.

All pure colors are intense in their natural form (photo 1). Once a small portion of gray is added to a color, it loses some of its visual strength. The more gray added, the less intense the color becomes. So, a strongly grayed color is low in intensity. The effect of graying a color is similar to placing a veil over it. The color becomes more unclear as the thickness of the gray veil increases (photos 2C, 27, 28, 35, 48, 53, 55, 78, 79).

Another word for intensity is *saturation*. If a color is pure, it is fully saturated, or high in saturation. If the strength of the color has been weakened by graying it, then its saturation has been weakened. An extremely grayed color is low in saturation. Fuchsia, a brilliant purplish red color, is fully saturated or high in saturation; dusty rose, a very grayed hue, is weak or low in saturation.

THE GLOW OF AN AFTERIMAGE

When you look at a color for any length of time, you begin to see another hue around its periphery. Sometimes the fleeting color seems to float on top of the original color; it can even linger on top of surrounding colors. This color phenomenon is called an *afterimage*. The afterimage of a color is always rather elusive in your mind's eye.

Every color has its own afterimage. This is a very pale tint derived from the hue's complementary color. In essence, a color and its afterimage represent a marriage of two colors that are in perfect harmony with each other. It is important to determine a color's afterimage when attempting to use this natural partnership to its fullest potential.

The afterimage of teal is a variation of apricot. The afterimage of forest green is a very light luminous pink. Mint green is the afterimage of bright fuchsia. The afterimage of a yellow may be a light periwinkle or lavender. Afterimages can vary somewhat among individual viewers, although the differences seem primarily to be associated with the value of the hue, rather than the actual color itself. (See photo 1 for pure color and afterimage partners.)

An afterimage is simply color leftovers. When light rays hit a surface, part of the light wave is reflected back to us as a specific color, like teal. The remaining rays are absorbed into the surface. These leftover light hues form the afterimage. In paint, when the root color and its afterimage are combined, a grayish color is formed. Using the two colors as partners can bring a feeling of completeness to art.

Using an Afterimage for an Accent

Consider using the afterimage as an accent color in your work. Look for small areas in a design that would be a good placement for an afterimage. It is beneficial to include the afterimage of your dominant color somewhere in the art, as it can help enhance the focal point, or strengthen the appearance of your dominant color. See photos 30, 40, 43, 47–49, 50–54, 73, and 80 for afterimage use.

If you create a landscape, try to include the afterimage of the dominant color family or focal point. If the sunlight is a dominant feature in your picture, use the afterimage either in the sky or somewhere in the foreground if possible (photo 31).

The strength of the afterimage is in its use as an accent. It adds vibrance and intensifies the beauty of colors. Simply stated, the afterimage completes the color partnership, helping to make your art a beautiful, whole entity.

Combining the Root Color with Its Afterimage

You may want to create work that uses a root color, its afterimage, and all the hues that fall between these two parent colors (photo 12). This total blend of colors makes a beautiful, harmonic statement. Generally, its emotive feel is quite restful.

When using this combination of colors, you need a transition between the root color and its afterimage. In paint you can make the transition by blending a drop of the afterimage into the root color. The root color then begins to gray. If you were to put a drop of the root color into the afterimage hue, there would also be a tonal cast on it. As you blend more of the opposite color into its partner, it becomes more toned. Eventually the two colors blend into a neutral grayish color that seems indistinguishable (figure 3-7).

Study the afterimage scale (photo 12). Notice that the root color and its afterimage contain no gray. As each color is added to the opposite one, however, the ensuing colors become more grayed, until a grayish, muddied color results. The brilliant pink, the root color, has no gray in it. It is high in intensity. Once grayed by the addition of the afterimage, the color loses its strength and its clarity, becoming less intense and low in saturation.

The hues used to blend a root color and its afterimage are transitional colors. Standing alone, they are usually visually unattractive. Although they may be considered drab colors, they are essential for building wonderful transitions between a root color and its afterimage. If you have a color that you are particularly fond of, determine its afterimage. Then collect the transitional colors for the partnership. These colors generally fail to

Root color

Green	1
Slightly grayed green	2
Lightly grayed green	3
Grayed green	4
Lightly greenish gray	5
Slightly greened gray	6
Mixture of green and pink– an indistinguishable gray	
Slightly pinkish gray	6
Lightly pinkish gray	5
Grayed pink	4
Lightly grayed pink	3
Slightly grayed pink	2
Clear pink	1

Afterimage

Figure 3-7 Combining a Root Color with Its Afterimage
To use a color and its afterimage in a design, each transitional hue must gradually move toward the neutral gray area in order to blend with the other color.

catch our eye on their own, but they are the key to creating fantastic color interactions, whether you work in fabric or another medium.

How To Find the Afterimage

It is easy to find the afterimages of your favorite colors. In an area of good light, place a white sheet of paper on a table. Then select a color for which you would like to find the afterimage. Cut out a small sample of this color from paper or fabric. A one- or two-inch square is ample. Put your color sample in the center of the white paper.

Stare at the colored sample for at least 15 to 30 seconds. As you stare at the color, notice a very light hue beginning to creep around the sides of the sample. This tint might even seem to move across the paper. After you have stared at the color for the specified time, remove the color sample from the white paper. While doing this, try not to blink or move. You should see a luminous tint appear in exactly the same configuration as the colored sample. Momentarily, this color may be quite bright, but after a few seconds it will fade away.

If you have trouble seeing the afterimage, stare at the colored paper for a longer period of time, for perhaps 30 to 60 seconds. If you wear glasses and have difficulty finding the afterimage, take them off. Then repeat the exercise.

Look at the two small colored figures (leaf and flower) in photo 11. Stare at the green leaf. Continue looking at it for at least 15 seconds or until you see a soft, luminous color surrounding it. Then, without blinking, focus your eyes on the black dot beside the color. You should see the afterimage of that particular hue. Notice that it repeats the exact size and configuration of the original color. Rest your eyes for a minute. Repeat the exercise, staring at the pink flower and then looking at the black dot to see the afterimage.

If you want to keep a notation of the actual color of a hue's afterimage, use the Letraset® Pantone Color Paper Selector (uncoated), paint chips, or colored paper samples. While you see the color image before you, quickly flip through the colors to find the one most similar. You may have to redo the exercise several times before you find the exact color within the color selectors. However, once you find the afterimage, you can cut a small piece from your colored paper. Use this sample when attempting to match the color.

CHEVREUL'S GIFT

In 1824 a unique opportunity was presented to Michel Eugene Chevreul, a brilliant young French chemist, that has, in effect, impacted the art world to this day. King Louis XVIII asked Chevreul to become the Director of Dyes for the Royal Manufacturers at Gobelins, the makers of the exquisite internationally renowned tapestries and carpets. Chevreul worked for almost three decades with the chemistry of dyes in his capacity of director at Gobelins.

As a result of Chevreul's discoveries and experiments, many of the world's most renowned painters have used his findings as their major color resource. Winslow Homer walked around with Chevreul's book in hand and considered it his bible. We, too, can use Chevreul's discoveries to our design advantage. His influence in the field of color is undisputed. Certainly he can be considered the forefather of modern color theory.

Basis for Discoveries

In his job as director, Chevreul worked with people who had purchased tapestries or carpets from Gobelins and who were dissatisfied with the product. Upon inspecting each written order and the resulting tapestry, Chevreul found that no mistake had been made in dyeing or creating the fiberwork. However, he did find that when these complaints occurred, there were, in fact, visual discrepancies between the order and the actual results. This led Chevreul to become curious about these recurring color problems.

Through careful observations, Chevreul found that color changes took place when certain color combinations were present. These changes created unusual visual illusions. Chevreul then experimented and found that he could duplicate the same effects in the laboratory. Eventually he could anticipate these troublesome color interactions; thus, he learned to recognize and control the visual problems inherent in some color combinations. His major discoveries, then, had to do with how colors interact in close proximity to each other. Chevreul's most important findings, which were originally brought to his attention by client dissatisfaction, are referred to as *simultaneous contrast* and *optical mixing.*

Through Chevreul's research and our own experiences, we know that colors are not static. Colors are similar to people—their personalities change and they can be influenced by close associations. So the placement of colors within a design, the interaction between neighboring hues, and the intensity of the colors all combine to affect the visual characteristics of a color.

Optical Mixing

When two different colors are placed side by side, the colors sometimes seem to blend into a new color. This happens especially when the art is viewed from a distance. This additional color is the average of the hue and value of the two parent colors (figure 3-8).

This blending of the parent colors into a new hue is not the result of physically mixing the colors. Instead, it is the consequence of our eyes and mind making a visual blend. This effect is called optical mixing. The result is a new optical color. Optical mixing is created through a type of personal additive color mixing. This effect creates a unity of color, whereby the similarities of two colors are strengthened and the differences are negated.

If you place small strips of green and blue colors side by side, your eyes may see a new color at the intersection line of the two. This new hue would be optically located somewhere between the two parent colors, perhaps a turquoise. The value of this new color would be a blend of the parent colors (photo 15A). When working with narrow strips of color, the optical blending occurs quite readily, allowing for greater beauty due to the additional colors your mind perceives. Quilts made with narrow strips of fabric often are enhanced by this illusion of optical mixing (photos 19, 30, 31, 37, 73).

Most optical mixing of colors results in hues that are less intense and more toned than the parent colors. This

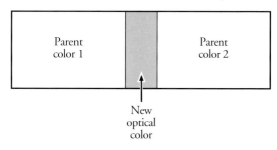

Figure 3-8 Optical Mixing
An optical color is the average of its parents in hue and value.

is because the eye cannot create intensity or brilliance from colors that are already grayed or have no close relationship (photos 15B, 15D). However, if you place together two intense colors that actually clash or are very close in hue, such as a fuchsia and red, the result is an optical mixing of the two hues which results in a new color of more vibrancy and intensity (photos 15A, 15C).

Optical mixing is not just a happenstance of two colors closely placed together. The effect of optical mixing also relies on the distance of the viewer from the art and the angle from which the art is seen. If you view the art at an angle, the optical mixing is more pronounced than if you view it straight on. If the viewer is too close or the size of the shapes or elements is too large, optical mixing may not occur.

If you view the art from too great a distance, the colors begin to lose their mixing qualities and tend to gray. The value of this gray depends on the parent colors' values. Light colors will become light gray; middle-value colors will become a middle tone; while dark colors will be more charcoal. If the parent colors have two different values, then the values will be a blend of both.

Simultaneous Contrast

Simultaneous contrast is a concept opposite to optical mixing. Instead of accentuating the similarities of colors, it intensifies the differences. The phenomenon is most pronounced when the hues, intensities, or values are at their greatest contrast. This contrast is greatly exaggerated by the presence of the afterimages.

The most pronounced visual effect occurs when light colors surround dark colors: the latter hues appear darker. Likewise, when light colors are surrounded by dark colors, they seem lighter than they actually are. In other words, each highly contrasting color brings out the opposite quality to its extreme. The effect reaches its maximum contrast when two complementary colors are positioned next to each other in their pure form (photos 14B, 14C).

Contrasts in other characteristics also bring about these optical differences. Warm colors look warmer

Continued on page 29

24

The Magical Effects of Color
Illustrations of Concepts

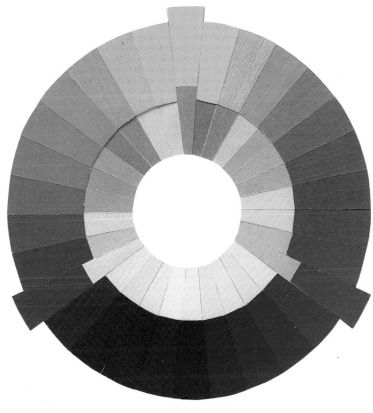

2. Color Scales.

(A-left) White added to pure color makes tints; (B-middle) black added, makes shades; (C-right) gray added, makes tones. See Chapter 2.

1. Color Wheel.

The pure color scale in 30 hues, with yellow, turquoise, and magenta as primary colors. Second ring of colors are the hues' afterimages. See Chapter 3.

3. Value Scale.

Colors move from highest values (lightest hues) to lowest values (darkest hues). Pure green and neutral gray narrow strips appear to change values as they move from one hue to another, showing color is relative. See Chapter 3.

Color studies 1–15 were created by Judith Prowse Buskirk and photographed by Ken Wagner.

A

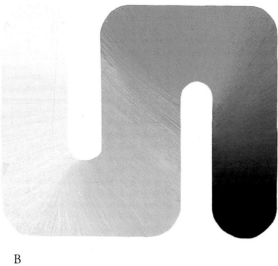

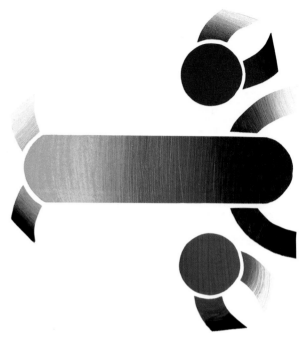

B

4. Monochromatic Color Scheme. Combination of tints, shades, tones, and pure color from one color family. Orange monochromatic color range shown. See Chapter 4.

5. Split-Complementary Color Scheme. Any three adjacent color families with the middle hue's complement. Magenta, purple, violet, and purple's complement, yellow-green shown along with their tints and shades. See Chapter 4.

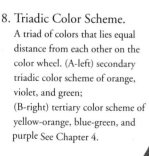

6. Complementary Color Scheme. Combination of hues from any two color families that lie opposite each other on the color wheel. Complements yellow and violet shown with their intermingled hues. See Chapter 4.

7. Analogous Color Scheme. A combination of any three color families adjacent to each other on the color wheel. Turquoise, blue-green, and green combined here. See Chapter 4.

8. Triadic Color Scheme.
A triad of colors that lies equal distance from each other on the color wheel. (A-left) secondary triadic color scheme of orange, violet, and green;
(B-right) tertiary color scheme of yellow-orange, blue-green, and purple See Chapter 4.

9. **Luminosity.** Colors that appear to glow are luminous. Colors need to be clear or less toned than the hues immediately surrounding them. See Chapter 5.

 .

10. **Luster.** Reflected light is lustrous. Closely related color values help achieve this effect. See Chapter 5.

11. **Afterimage.** An afterimage is a color's most complete partner. To find, stare at the leaf for 15–30 seconds. Without blinking, focus on nearby dot. Afterimage color will appear in identical size and shape. Repeat steps to find flower afterimage. See Chapter 3.

12. **Afterimage Scale.**
Grass green and its afterimage become toned as they blend together. See Chapter 3.

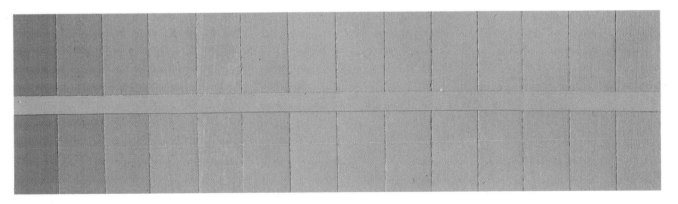

13. Transparency.

Three types of transparency can be achieved:
(A) both colors appear transparent; (B and C)
transparent color appears as film over opaque
color underneath; (D and E) transparent
color appears floating above an opaque hue.
See Chapter 6.

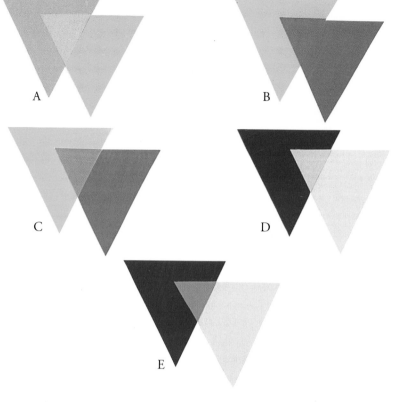

14. Simultaneous Contrast.

Colors are influenced by surrounding hues,
particularly if strongly contrasted: (A-left)
cool color (turquoise) surrounded by a warm
color (yellow) appears cool; when surrounded
by a cooler color (purple), it appears warm;
(B-middle) colors appear more intense when
they contrast in temperature; (C-right) colors
appear more intense when with their pure
complement. See Chapter 3.

15. Optical Mixing: (A and C) Small amounts of clashing colors of high intensity can add new vibrant colors to the design through optical mixing where colors meet. (B and D) Optical mixing of toned hues is more subtle. See Chapter 3.

A   B   C   D

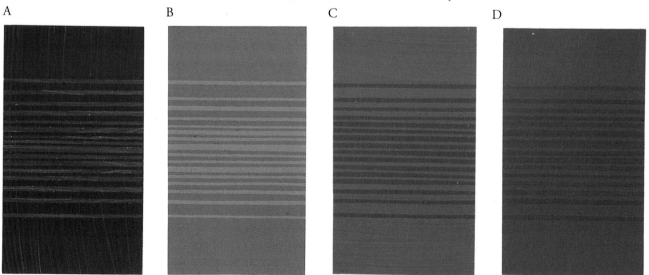

28

Continued from page 24

adjacent to cool colors (photos 14B–C, 17, 42, 66, 73). The reverse is also true: cool colors look cooler in the presence of warm colors (photos 14B–C, 17, 25). Pure colors seem more intense next to toned hues. Grayed colors seem more toned next to highly intense colors.

EMPHASIZING SIMULTANEOUS CONTRAST IN YOUR ARTWORK

If you are interested in creating simultaneous contrast in your artwork, several methods help promote this effect. You can use complementary colors in their purest forms. If you do, make the shapes large enough so that the eye can see the space clearly. The eye will automatically see the afterimage, thereby intensifying its root color and the complement. You can also intensify two colors by using strong value differences.

To promote simultaneous contrast, you can use relatively small toned areas in the background while the foreground is made up of large, intense formations. To accentuate even further, use toned afterimage hues. This, of course, intensifies the differences between the two colors. A black background increases the drama and intensity of colors. Using the most intense pure colors, of course, will accentuate the differences.

REDUCING THE POSSIBILITY OF SIMULTANEOUS CONTRAST

There may be times when you wish to use colors that would cause simultaneous contrast, but you want to reduce the effects rather than encourage them. There are a few ways to do this. The most intense colors and strongest contrasts produce the strongest afterimages. To weaken the afterimage or eliminate it, use hues of low intensity or with very little value contrasts.

Using complements in large amounts increases simultaneous contrast; using the complements in small amounts diminishes the effect because the afterimage doesn't have enough space to show itself. The afterimage effect can be stopped by outlining those shapes that will be affected with white, black, or gray. Similarly, you can separate the colored shapes that would reflect afterimages by large areas of neutral colors (including lattice work). Also, if you place small shapes of black and white throughout your design, it seems to eliminate simultaneous contrast because your eyes rest on them rather than concentrating on the other colors.

UNINTENTIONAL AFTERIMAGES

If you are creating an artwork that has an extremely strong dominant color among other less intense colors on a gray background, sometimes the afterimage of the strong hue will inadvertently come forward in the artwork. When this happens, it often appears to overlap or mingle with the other hues. This can result in a unified feeling. At other times, the afterimage of a strong hue may play with the other colors in such a way that an illusion of transparency results. Both of these inadvertent playings of the afterimage on the surface of the design are difficult to predict or plan.

Sometimes when there are many strong pure hues on a grayed background, the afterimages of many of the colors superimpose themselves across the surface. This may be particularly pronounced if the artwork is viewed in strong light. This particular afterimage play can cause distraction and discomfort in the artwork, which may or may not be welcomed by the artist.

If the strong hues are complementary to each other, the afterimages will also be complementary. This blending of the afterimage with the main hues can cause really interesting blends of color. The visual blending appears fleetingly to the viewer, or the blending may constantly shift. The effect is not based on actual colors, but on the visual perception created by our eyes and our mind. This visual play with a root color and its afterimage can result in very beautiful blends of color. Again, neither of these afterimage plays is very predictable. If the artwork is placed in dim light, the afterimages will most likely be seen quite quickly and then fade immediately. When the art is placed in more brilliant light, the afterimage will seem more intense and will be visible for a longer period of time.

"... There is a lot to painting that can't be explained and which is essential. You arrive in front of Nature with theories, and Nature throws them to the ground."

"Composition should be as varied as nature."

—Pierre Auguste Renoir
French painter, 1841–1919
The Impressionists

CHAPTER 4

Nature and Color—A Symphony of Hues

The great art that we see and the art we wish to create all begin from the same points of reference: an individual's creative ideas, emotions, intuition, observations, experimentation, discovery, and acquired knowledge. All these points of reference are reflected in the colors one brings together to create a work of art. Therefore, it is important that we know the color options available to us and are able to choose those that best communicate the visual message we wish to convey. For these basic color choices, we can again look toward nature.

Through the ages, artists have carefully observed nature's blending of hues, taking note that each natural play of color leads to beautiful outcomes. Nature's choices range from the most subtle combinations to the most dramatic. Her diversity in color use can be categorized into five major color plans, although other minor ones also exist. These natural color schemes are described here, providing you with visual images, basic information, options, and ideas for your own use. Use these plans as guidelines rather than restrictive rules. Your unique ideas, emotions, and creative needs should always take precedence over generalized rules.

ELEGANCE AND SIMPLICITY: THE MONOCHROMATIC COLOR SCHEME

The midday blue sky above us is the largest natural element based on one color family—the monochromatic color scheme. In its simplest form, blue sky variations change from light to dark or bright to gray. Vast forests are also lovely examples of the monochromatic color scheme, with a mantle of luscious green covering the earth as far as one can see. Innumerable flowers use the monochromatic color scheme too, often displaying a gentle gradation within one color family. Scores of birds are monochromatically colored, with their variations of color depending on value and intensity. All are exquisite in their simple coloring. The quiet beauty of this color plan is amplified by the changes that take place as the hues are muted, intensified, deepened, or softened.

Requirements of a Monochromatic Color Scheme

In a monochromatic color scheme the colors in a design all come from the same color family. This is the simplest of all color combinations, yet it can create a strong feeling of sophisticated elegance. Although it can be dramatically beautiful, the monochromatic color scheme can be difficult to use successfully. Because its most important ingredient is value, you must incorporate value changes in your design. Diversity of value adds beauty, richness, and strength to monochromatic coloration. Any hue can be lightened or darkened. Within a color family, the range of colors between a blush white and the darkest hue is immense (figure 4-1, photos 4, 62, 71, 86).

In some designs, interest and beauty can be enhanced by changing the intensity of the colors. Graying the hues can be quite effective, particularly if the tones are varied in the degree of their intensity (photo 60). The focal-point hue may be quite strong visually, but interest and movement may be achieved by using a tonal scale ranging from the purest colors to the grayest hues (photos 2C, 4B).

Values and the Monochromatic Color Scheme

Because values are the most important element in monochromatic artwork, it is important to remember how values function in art. Think of degrees of value as stair steps going from the darkest hue to the lightest. The darkest colors are at the bottom of the stairs, and the highest steps are the lightest in value. Often the lowest values give the most weight, acting like an anchor, while the highest values are airy and fantasy-like, seeming to float above all else (photos 3, 86).

To ensure interest and variation, try to include at least seven to nine value steps in your monochromatic theme. Commonly, the value scale is divided into nine steps: white, high light, light, low light, middle, high dark, dark, low dark, and black. Depending on the color family you work with, the pure color will be at a different step on the value scale (figure 3-6).

In the monochromatic color scheme, excellent results are attained if you use closely graduated values. These are any three consecutive values along the value scale. The values can change within the art, but the changes are very subtle because they are made in gentle steps. Working with analogous values in this color scheme can promote quiet beauty (photo 60).

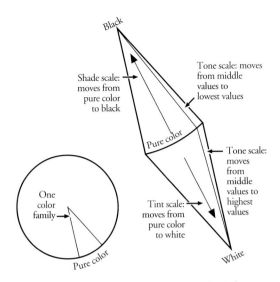

Figure 4-1 The Monochromatic Color Scheme
The monochromatic color scheme uses hues from only one color family. The hues in the design can incorporate pure colors, tints, shades, and tones in a multitude of values.

If you place contrasting values together in this theme, you elicit a much different emotional response. The work will appear more dramatic. For instance, placing a high light and a low dark together will be quite striking, as they are the most contrasting values except for white and black.

How To Use the Monochromatic Color Scheme

Before beginning your artwork, decide on the mood you want to create. Then choose the color family you intend to use to elicit this mood. Determine which hues in the family you will use. Decide whether you will use only value changes in your design, or work primarily with intensity changes, or combine both value and intensity changes.

When creating art, analogous values are well placed in background areas or in large open spaces. These subtle gradations allow interesting interminglings of color. However, use values of highest contrast where you want your design focus. These high-contrast areas define the major area of interest.

Troubleshooting Problems with the Monochromatic Color Scheme

Too many nonrelated, highly contrasting values can be distracting in a monochromatic color scheme. The eye doesn't know where to rest, so it jumps from element to element. If you work with highly contrasting values, place them in your design so that they move the eye across the art.

Sometimes you may find that your artwork lacks drama or spunk. When this happens, do not abandon the color scheme. The problem very likely lies in the lack of value changes. Value changes allow the design to be seen. Try making stronger value changes than you have, perhaps moving the values a step or two away from the dominant value, and see how that affects the total design.

Beautiful Harmony: The Analogous Color Scheme

Nature often uses a very harmonic color scheme which employs three closely related hues. This is called an *analogous color scheme*. Because of the harmony of the colors used, an analogous color scheme is one of the most beautiful for an artwork.

Often we are treated to a beautiful, analogously colored sunrise, with yellows, apricots, and peaches gently unfolding into a graceful design, seemingly painted with delicate strokes across the eastern sky. Bodies of water can be another source of analogous coloration. On close inspection, you will find that daytime water is not just blue, but may range from green, to blue-green, to blue. At other times, the range may begin at blue-green and lead into blue and periwinkle, a purplish blue. This blending of closely related colors adds sparkle and richness to the water.

Many flowers display their colors in an analogous color scheme. One of the most notable, the exquisitely colored Chicago Peace rose, moves from yellow to copper to a deep pink. The familiar daffodil is often analogous in coloration. The yellow flower's center is often orange, while yellow-green softly blends petals and stem together. Many animals, birds, and insects also exhibit colorings of the analogous color scheme. For instance, the wings of some butterflies are a beautiful display of purple, violet, and blue mingled together.

Requirements of an Analogous Color Scheme

The analogous color scheme uses three closely related color families that are placed side by side on the color wheel (photo 7). Any three adjacent colors can be used. Each of these color families is related to the others because they have a similar color component. Examples of adjacent colors are: (1) yellow, yellow-green, green; (2) yellow-green, green, blue-green; (3) green, blue-green, turquoise; (4) blue-green, turquoise, blue; (5) turquoise, blue, violet; (6) blue, violet, purple; (7) violet, purple, magenta; (8) purple, magenta, red; (9) magenta, red, orange; (10) red, orange, yellow-orange; (11) orange, yellow-orange, yellow; and (12) yellow-orange, yellow, and yellow-green (photos 1, 7; figure 4-2). An analogous scheme may also include a more generalized group of these colors, as in yellow, green, and blue (photo 22).

In an analogous color scheme, additional color variations can be achieved by changing the color values. The hues can span from tints to the pure color through the

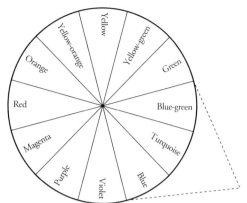

Figure 4-2 The Analogous Color Scheme
An analogous color scheme uses hues from any three colors that lie next to each other on the color wheel. The hues in the design can include pure colors, tints, shades, and tones.

shades. If one of your analogous colors was yellow, the total range of hues could run from creams to pure yellow, and then to the olives. Intensity changes can also provide color variety. Use a variety of toned hues in each color family. For example, if you use red, magenta, and purple, you could include numerous roses and mauves. Art created in the analogous color scheme includes photos 37, 39, 78, 79, 81, 82, and 84.

How To Use the Colors in an Analogous Color Scheme

Of three adjacent colors, choose one to be the dominant hue, another to be the secondary color, and the third to be the accent. One successful method of using the analogous color scheme is to choose the most intense color, or the purest, for the accent color. The surrounding colors should be less intense, perhaps toned or shaded. The purest hue, or accent, would be the brightest and most pronounced color, advancing visually more than the others. (If the surrounding colors are close in tone and value to the pure accent, the result will not be as dramatic as if the surrounding colors contrast in value or intensity.) A pure accent color should never compete for dominance. If its strength gives too much visual impact, lessen its use or make it less intense. The dominant color should always retain the visual strength.

Effects of an Analogous Color Scheme

Nature regularly demonstrates one of the most exciting attractions of the analogous color scheme. When adjacent colors are placed beside one another, each interacts with the others to add depth or brilliance to the overall appearance. The vibrant, striking colors of autumn leaves are an example of this. Alone, each color appears rather common. Yet when these colors mingle, each reinforces the others and makes the totality more brilliant than the individual parts. Even quite grayed or subdued colors exhibit richness when placed together

with adjacent colors. This mingling of adjacent colors adds a sparkle and depth that is hard to achieve otherwise.

ANALOGOUS COLOR SCHEME AND MIST OR FOG

The analogous color scheme works well to create a feeling of mistiness or fog in your art. All your colors should be very toned. This toning effect, if properly applied, gives the feel of wintery weather, mist, fog, or mystery. The more the colors are grayed, the more atmospheric the effect becomes (photo 26).

OPPOSITES ATTRACT—THE COMPLEMENTARY COLOR SCHEME

If you watch sunsets, you will be amazed how often they come in complementary color schemes—hues that lie opposite each other on the color wheel. Often creams and yellows intermix with violets, lavenders, and purples in the sky. A common yet extremely beautiful blend of colors in the early evening sky is oranges and apricots with blue. Many sunsets seem to revolve around these two color families and their complements, treating us to limitless variations on the same theme.

More often than not, blue and violet flowers contrast exquisitely with centers of orange and yellow, respectively. Irises are marvelous examples of using violet and yellow together in stunning brilliance. Pink dogwood, as well as numerous other spring flowering trees, shower us with pink blossoms and fresh green leaves in delicate hues. Likewise, many birds and butterflies are strikingly colored with complementary blue and orange.

Requirements of a Complementary Color Scheme

The major complementary color scheme partners are: (1) yellow and violet; (2) orange and turquoise; (3) magenta and green; (4) red and blue–green; and (5) blue and yellow–orange. Each partnership has its own personality and visual characteristics. If you are attracted to one of these color combinations or if it fits perfectly with the mood you are trying to create, use these natural partners as your color guide (photos 1, 6; figure 4-3).

These pairs in their purest forms may be the least becoming combinations, yet it is often the way we visualize this form of color partnership. Their real beauty blossoms when the colors are mingled together. The result is a lovely blend of new hues in subtle tones (photo 6). For examples of art done in the complementary color scheme, see photos 17, 25, 27, 54, and 70.

MIXING COMPLEMENTARY COLORS

It's difficult to visualize the possibilities achieved through mixing complementary partners if you have never had the opportunity to mix colors with paints. If possible, take time to play with paints, investigating

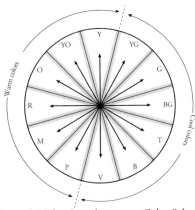

Figure 4-3 The Complementary Color Scheme
The complementary color scheme includes all the pure hues, tints, tones, and shades of the color partners that lie opposite each other on the color wheel. The partners in a 12-step color wheel include: yellow/violet; yellow-green/purple; green/magenta; blue-green/red; turquoise/orange; and blue/yellow-orange. As each color changes its hue slightly by moving closer to the adjacent hue, its complement also shifts slightly. For example, a green near the green/blue-green border will have a complement that will verge on a blued red at the magenta/red border. Shaded areas along the color borders illustrate these potential shiftings.

color possibilities in your artwork. See photo 6 for a beautiful complementary blend of yellow and violet.

When you add a small amount of complementary color to its partner, it becomes slightly gray. The more complementary color added, the more the root color grays. Eventually the combination of the two becomes an indistinguishable grayed color, the pair's neutral. If you mix complementary partners in paint, notice that when the two hues are not thoroughly mixed, but are just mingled together, the outcome can have a vibrant effect. The vibrance is somewhat elusive, and much prettier than when the two colors are completely mixed (photo 6).

EFFECTS OF A COMPLEMENTARY COLOR SCHEME

When choosing colors, don't restrict yourself merely to exact opposites on the color wheel. These opposing forces can be too strong or harsh to be artistically pleasing. If you are using yellow and violet, include hues that mingle into yellow-orange, yellow-green, blue-violet, and red-violet. This neighborly mingling should not upset the balance of the complementary color scheme, nor should it change the basic coloration. Instead, it should enhance the beauty of your design (photos 53, 58, 70).

YELLOW AND VIOLET PARTNERS

The complementary partners yellow and violet have a very special relationship. Each of these colors lies adjacent to the warm and cool relative boundary on the color wheel (figure 4-3). Therefore, often their partnership is not so intense as the other major partnerships, which have one partner definitely in the warm side and the other hue in the cool side.

Yellow is the color most associated with light and sunlight, and violet is most associated with shadows and darkness. This combination of colors is particularly useful for creating artwork that includes the complete spectrum from sunlight to deep shadows.

Pure yellow is considered three times as bright as violet. Therefore, for violet to visually overpower an intense yellow, an artwork would have to contain far more violet than its counterpart (photos 54, 66). To be more dominant, violet would have to cover more than three times the surface area of a yellow in the same intensity range. If the intensity or value of violet was weaker or lighter than the yellow, the ratio would have to be even greater. Yellow carries great attraction in its purest form.

TURQUOISE AND ORANGE PARTNERS

Turquoise and orange, two other complementary colors, elicit the extremes of hot and cold (photos 17, 25). Orange is almost twice as bright as turquoise in value. Therefore, to make turquoise the dominant color, it would have to cover at least twice as much surface as orange does in its purest form. However, toning down the orange and intensifying the turquoise can change the ratio to turquoise's favor.

MAGENTA AND GREEN PARTNERS

Magenta and green are nearly equal in value on the color wheel. Thus, their partnership emphasizes the optical intensity they can promote with each other. For visual ease, one color must be made the dominant partner.

Using a Complementary Color Scheme

Often we visualize using complementary colors at full strength. Doing so can make a harsh visual statement that completely overwhelms the eye. Therefore, it is important to control the strong pure colors with large areas of toned colors—those that have been grayed to a

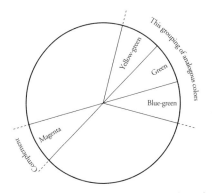

Figure 4-4 The Split-Complementary Color Scheme
A split-complementary color scheme is a combination of an analogous color scheme and a complementary color scheme. The complement is the partner of the middle analogous color. It can be an accent, the dominant color, or can have a role somewhere between the two extremes.

variety of intensities in the complementary family. If you can harmonize the strong colors with complementary neutrals, your artwork will contain both zest and beauty.

It is important to decide which of two complementary colors will be dominant. When both colors fight for dominance, it leads to discomfort for the viewer. Once you choose the dominant color, use the subordinate one to help give the design visual balance.

If you decide to use complementary colors to enhance color movement, as in woven bands, then wherever they cross each other's paths, the colors should be deeply intensified—much more so than if they were set in a design that showed no movement (photo 70).

BLENDING HARMONY & CONTRAST: SPLIT–COMPLEMENTARY COLOR SCHEME

Many times landscapes are cast in a blend of analogous colors with a complement that adds not only interest, but a temperature shift. Cool evening landscape colors are often accentuated by a warm sky above. In the springtime garden the blue-green, green, and yellow-green mantle of leaves moves gracefully among the flourishing pink blossoms of trees and shrubs, contrasting beautifully.

Requirements of a Split-Complementary Color Scheme

Although the split-complementary color scheme is one of the most beautiful in nature, we rarely seem to use this plan in our art. It has the advantage of bringing together closely related colors of the analogous color scheme with one set of complementary hues. This contrasting set of colors comes from the complement of the middle analogous color (figure 4-4 and photo 5). We often see this color scheme in a landscape setting, with the distant hills cast in violet, violet-blue, and blue, while blue-violet's complement, yellow-orange, offers a contrast in the evening sky.

The complement adds a harmonious balance. If the pure hue is used, it is usually just a small accent. The more subtle the contrasting color, the more area this color can encompass with pleasing effects. See photo 5 for an example of a split-complementary color scheme, with magenta, purple, and violet as analogous colors, and yellow-green as the complementary hue. Shades and tints of each hue have been included.

One of the wonderful characteristics of this color scheme is that it is so versatile in creating a variety of moods. By changing the dominant color, the values, and the intensities, you can take the same design and create incredibly different effects. This, then, is an extremely

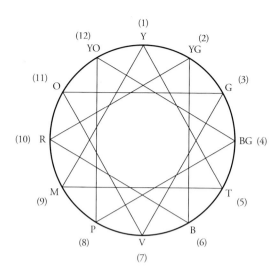

Figure 4-5 The Triadic Color Scheme
Triadic color schemes use colors positioned equally around the color wheel. In a 12-step color wheel, the color trios are four colors apart. On the color wheel, lines are drawn to connect the three colors. There are four triadic color schemes shown here: primary, secondary, and two tertiary combinations.

exciting color scheme to work in (photos 33, 38, 43, 75–77).

Using the Split-Complementary Color Scheme

If you would like to use this color scheme, decide what mood you wish your artwork to convey. From that, pick your three analogous colors. The middle color will determine the opposite color. Its complement will act as a visual balance. Most often the complement will be used as an accent, but its role is not restricted to this. It is difficult for the contrasting hue to be made into the dominant color and, consequently, the dominant temperature. However, it can be done successfully with planning.

For additional interest and beauty, change the values of the colors used. The family of colors in the analogous group and the complement can range from delicate lightness to the dimness of pervading darkness. As well, the colors can range from pure intensity to subtle tones. When you create a design with this scope, the purest color often becomes the focus in the design.

The three analogous color families cannot be allowed to compete with each other for dominance. Each must play a role and keep to that position: one will be dominant, another secondary, and the third takes a lesser role, perhaps even as the accent. The complementary hue must also be placed appropriately in its own role, whether it be a mere accent, or holds a stronger position. As you plan your design, attempt to move the colors across the composition so that your eye is led from one area to the next.

UNLIKELY PARTNERS: THE TRIADIC COLOR SCHEME

Sometimes nature blends colors beautifully in a seemingly unrelated grouping. These blendings can be subtle or vibrant, depending on the combination used. Rocks of subtle green, violet, and orange are not unusual. Some of the most spectacular sunsets mingle yellow, blue, and magenta across the sky in strong streaks. From a Pacific Ocean beach it's not uncommon to see color combinations of orange, green, and violet in the sky. Even certain leaves can be a triadic mixture of greens, violets, and oranges within the top surface, the underside, and the veins. These beautiful blendings use the triadic color scheme.

Requirements of a Triadic Color Scheme

In a triadic color scheme you use any three colors that are of equal distance from each other on the color wheel. On a twelve-step color wheel each color within a triad would include every fourth color (figure 4-5). The most dynamic of these color triads is yellow, turquoise, and magenta—the three primaries. This color plan is at its best when there are definite value changes ranging from light to dark.

When working with a triadic color scheme, choose one color to be the dominant hue, another to be secondary, and the third to be the accent. In some triadic combinations you have two warm colors and one cool color. In other sets, the reverse is true. It is usually easiest to take your dominant color from the dominant temperature. Although it's harder to accomplish, you can successfully create an artwork using the color from the contrasting temperature as the dominant color.

If you are interested in working with triadic color designs, consider mixing watercolors or acrylics to familiarize yourself with these blended trios. You will discover beautiful colorations that can be achieved with triadic color schemes. With the choices of three possible

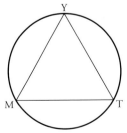

Figure 4-6 The Primary Triadic Color Scheme
This color scheme incorporates the three primary colors yellow, magenta, and turquoise. Additionally, all colors created by blending these three colors may also be included (secondary and tertiary colors). These colors may be tinted, shaded, and toned. The primary triadic color combination could be an overwhelming amount of colors if not well thought out.

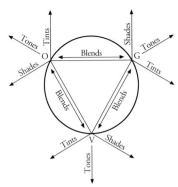

Figure 4-7 The Secondary Triadic Color Scheme
The secondary triadic color scheme uses green, violet, and orange as its color combination. Tints, shades, and tones of those colors can also be used. The main beauty of this combination comes from the blend of colors that results when the pairs of colors are combined. This triadic combination is predominantly a cool temperature design with green and violet being cool and orange being warm.

dominant colors in a triad design and the options of a myriad of neutralized colors between the three sets, you can create innumerable designs beginning from the same three colors.

The Primary Triadic Color Scheme

The most difficult triad with which to create a beautiful design is the primary one (figure 4-6). The problem is that when this triad of colors is mixed together, the result is a combination of all the colors in the color wheel—the primary, secondary, and tertiary colors, including their tints, shades, and tones (photo 1). This can become a confusing mass of colors to work with, especially if you are inexperienced at color blending. Artwork using the primary triadic color scheme in several different types of blending can be seen in photos 19, 21, 23, 41, and 44–46.

The primary triadic color scheme can be extremely strong when worked in the pure form. Colors used in full intensity can be disastrous if the design is not carefully planned. Changing the values and tones of the hues can be the most important element in creating a beautiful design with this triad (photo 44).

In this particular triadic combination, if magenta and yellow are warm and turquoise is cool, it would be easiest to have one of the warm colors dominant. However, if the magenta leans toward the cool side, the temperature may shift, giving you different options for your dominant color.

The Secondary Triadic Color Scheme

The secondary triadic color plan is much more subtle than the clear, intense hues of the primary triadic mixture. It is made up of green, violet, and orange (figure 4-7; photo 8A). These secondary colors can be used as pure colors; or they can include tints and shades, changing from light to dark; or they can incorporate a wide variety of tones (photo 30). The beauty of this combination comes from the blend of colors that results when orange and green, green and violet, and violet and orange are combined into intermingled hues.

Because green and violet are often cool colors and orange is a warm color, this triad can easily be designed as predominantly cool. A design could include the violet family as the dominant colors, grayed greens as the secondary colors, and accents of apricot, grayed oranges, a touch of clearer orange, or even a bit of coral. This can be a very pleasing, subtle coloration.

Tertiary Triadic Color Scheme

There are two tertiary color schemes in a twelve-step color wheel (figure 4-8). One is the combination of yellow-green, blue, and red (photo 68). The other is the combination of blue-green, purple, and yellow-orange (photos 8B, 29). Both of these combinations result in the mixture of beautiful hues. Each can exhibit a wide array of hues that vary in moods.

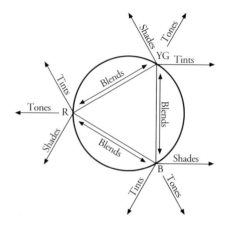

Figure 4-8 The Tertiary Triadic Color Scheme (B)
Beautiful hues result from the mixture of yellow-green, blue, and red (the blue leans toward violet and the red leans toward orange).

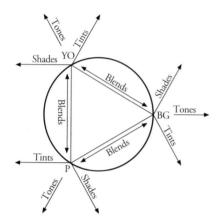

Figure 4-8 The Tertiary Triadic Color Scheme (A)
Beautiful hues result from the combination of yellow-orange, blue-green, and purple.

"The expressive side of color imposes itself upon me in a purely instinctive way. In order to show a fall landscape, I will not try to recall the particular nuances of that season; instead I will draw solely on the feelings that autumn has aroused in me . . . My sensation can vary depending on my observations, feelings, and sensory experiences. An artist like Signac is concerned with complementary color and his theoretical knowledge of this area will impel him to use certain colors here and there. As for me, I simply try to employ the colors that render a sensation."

–Henri Matisse
French painter, 1869–1954
"Notes of a Painter"
La Grande Revue
December 25, 1908

CHAPTER 5

Creating Exciting Light Effects

In our world of color we are captivated by light and all its elusive qualities. The impression of light created through art can bring us sparkle, glow, luster, three-dimensionality, shadows, highlights, iridescence, and opalescence. The illusionary qualities of light through color manipulation challenge our abilities, knowledge, and imagination. You can create an extraordinarily beautiful work of art by incorporating one of these intriguing illusions. Enjoy the challenging journey into light exploration.

LUMINOSITY

Luminosity is the ability to glow or to appear to glow. This glowing quality can be both manmade and natural. You can easily create a luminous effect by using nature's simple guidelines. Size of the glow, the value differences between the glow and the surrounding hues, and the intensity of the colors used are all important elements for attaining luminosity. See figure 5-1 and photo 9 for examples of luminosity.

To us, the sun is the largest luminous element in nature. The light of a candle gives a luminous glow, as does the light from a window late at night. The moon is perceived as luminous although it is not a self-glowing entity. Instead, light from the sun reflects on it. However, because the moon is so brilliantly lit by the sun, we think of it as glowing.

Size of Glow

Visualize the different luminous objects mentioned above—the sun, a candle, or a lighted window. In real life, they each appear as a small element within a total field of vision. For instance, the sun or moon is cast against a total landscape scene. A candle's flame is small in comparison to its total setting. A window, glowing from within, is a very small part of a total structure.

There is a visual ratio between our perception of a glow and its size. The farther back we stand from an element, the more it seems to glow. The closer we are to it, the more it becomes part of the total lighting that surrounds us. In most cases, then, the larger the glow becomes, the less effective it will be. Therefore, the glow in your art should not overwhelm the field with its size. If the luminous effect is too large, it simply looks like a

Figure 5-1 Luminosity and Luster
The sun is luminous, or self-glowing. The water is lustrous, reflecting the sun's light.

value change rather than luminosity. Placing a glowing effect in one small area or incorporating many tiny areas of luminosity throughout the entire field can be very successful in a design (photos 43, 44, 47, 64, 73, 85).

Value

Luminosity generally occurs in dim light or darkness. To achieve luminosity, there must be a difference between the value of the glowing area and that of the background or the rest of the field. For instance, when a candle burns in bright daylight, the glow is hardly apparent. However, if you take that same candle into a darkened room, the flame glows brilliantly. The contrast in value does not have to be strong, but it does have to be visually apparent.

Color Intensity

The glow is made up of colors that are clearer or less grayed (toned) than those colors immediately surrounding it. The glowing area can actually be made from grayed hues, as long as the surrounding colors have a greater degree of grayness (photo 85). Often the glow is made up of tints or pure colors. The less luminous areas should be weaker in saturation, thereby being somewhat grayed. The surrounding area is made up of toned hues. The glow, then, is made from the intensity change between the tones from the surrounding area and the clearer colors of the glow (photos 43, 44, 64, 85).

Many different hues can mix together to form a luminous area. Sunrises and sunsets are good examples of luminosity. When you look at a sunset, notice that the areas that glow, whether the sun or glowing streaks in the sky, are quite clear of gray. The areas immediately surrounding the glow are, in contrast, toned.

Colors which Are Easiest To Make Glow

The hues that are lightest or highest in value are the easiest to make glow. Yellow is the highest valued color, meaning that it is the color closest to white; so it will be the easiest hue to use for luminosity. Yellow-oranges and yellow-greens are the next highest in value, and thus are also relatively easy to make glow. The most difficult colors to create luminosity with are blues, purples, and violets, because these colors are so low in value. This does not mean, however, that these hues cannot glow—only that it is a more difficult task to achieve than with lighter valued colors.

Creating Luminosity in Your Artwork

Luminosity is a wonderful illusion to create. It can easily be created using small areas of hue changes, going from the clearest colors to those that increase their tonal quality. In your design, decide what would be the most appropriate element for a luminous effect. Then select the hues and fabrics you will use in this area. Be certain that colors used for the glow are free from gray or are less grayed than the surrounding hues. Next, choose the surrounding tonal colors and their placement in the design.

Designs with large elements (pattern pieces) may have to be divided into smaller units to create the illusion of luminosity effectively (photo 85).

LUSTER

Luster is sometimes confused with luminosity. These two illusions are similar; however, they have important differences. Lustrous objects do not radiate light from within as luminous entities do. Rather, a light from another source shines onto the object, giving it a sheen. Luster can be a soft reflected light, or it can be highly intense, dramatic, and colorful.

Light falling on snow or light reflecting onto a lake are examples of luster. A Christmas tree ball is lustrous when a tree light shines on it. A highly waxed table may show luster. Even parts of our fingernails can appear lustrous when light hits them. The mingling hues of flowers are often created by the lustrous effect of the sunlight striking their soft petals. For examples of luster, see figure 5-1 and photo 10.

Requirements

As with luminosity, in order to attain luster the background often appears dim, dark, or in shadow; there should be a definite value difference between the background and the lustrous object. The background for the lustrous effect is generally made of shades when the design is in middle or low key. For high-keyed art, luster is often created with tints or high-valued tones.

Luster is achieved by subtly changing the values of a color as it moves through the design. This value change creates the impression that light hits an object where the highest value exists (photos 21, 54). The strongest luster is created when the colors range from the lightest tint to the deepest shade. The impression of light hitting ribbons of fabric can even be created (photos 60, 70, 83).

For a soft lustrous effect, the colors start with a tint or very high-valued tone and decrease in value through the tone scale of that particular hue (photos 48, 49, 60). The darkest value used will depend on the design's value key. For instance, luster in a snow scene will probably remain relatively high in its values.

Although luster is made up of color gradations, these color steps do not have to be perfect gradations. The hues can be uneven in their value steps. They may also clash (photo 72). The values will move either from light to dark or from dark to light. This movement can repeat itself in reverse order for some designs (photos 60, 71).

Like luminosity, luster is only really effective when it takes up a relatively small portion of the entire area. It loses its identity if it is so large it overwhelms the field.

Creating Luster in Your Artwork

A most effective way to use luster is to create a design that expresses light hitting certain sections of it (photos 30, 33, 42). Designs that show three-dimensionality are wonderful with luster. Curved ribbons, interwoven elements, and geometric forms are all excellent formats for experimenting with lustrous effects (photos 17, 45, 46, 70, 75, 76, 83). Landscapes showing the sun or moon reflecting on a surface also make great settings for luster.

An overall design can be an effective composition for using luster. The colors can be positioned to move from one end to another in value changes. Even the colorations in traditional blocks can be placed across the surface of the design in a way that achieves luster.

SHADOWS AND HIGHLIGHTS

Shadows and highlights can be integral parts of a work of art. They are closely related to each other, as each belongs to the opposite end of the spectrum of light values. Shadows appear when light is diminished, and highlights are created when light is brilliantly present.

Figure 5-2A Strong Light Sharply Defines Shadows

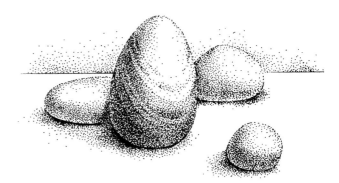

Figure 5-2B Diffused Light Promotes Blurred Shadows

Shadows

It is easiest to understand shadows if you go outside to observe them. Study those created by trees, utility poles, birds, houses, and other structures. Then study shadows inside your home. Observe shadows at different times of day and in different environments.

When an object casts a shadow from a single source of strong light, like the sun or a lamp, most often the edges of the shadow are strongly defined. If a shadow is formed simply with light that spreads through an entire area, the shadow edges are softly blurred (figures 5-2A, 2B).

When you see your own shadow, notice that your shadow feet and lower legs are fairly well formed. The line definition is quite sharp. However, as your shadow echoes the upper part of your body it becomes distorted. The shadow becomes more blurred as it moves farther away from the shadow's point of origin, your feet, at ground level.

The same is true for a tree. In summer, the trunk shadow is well defined while the far branches and leaves are unclear and blurred. In winter, when the leaves are gone, the shadow of the tree trunk and nearest branches are the most defined and darkest in color. The tallest branches are not only less defined, but are also more toned. As the shadow moves away from the object, it loses its strength and becomes lighter (figure 5-3).

When the sun is low in the sky, shadows are elongated. When the sun is high in the sky, they are shortened. The closer the light source is to the shadowed object, the larger the shadow cast. Likewise, the farther away the light is, the smaller the shadow will be.

If you look at shadows cast by both distant and nearby objects at the same time, you will see two different types of shadows. The shadow cast by the nearby object will be more clearly defined, with relatively hard edges. The shadow cast by an object farther away will be more blurred.

Indoors, shadows caused by highly diffused light, such as daylight, will appear soft and blurred, almost melting into each other. The shadowed colors are subtle and not highly contrasted. Shadows caused by direct sunlight will be sharply edged and more highly contrasting.

Colors of a Shadow

A shadow is strongest when bright light is present. In order to create the illusion of a shadow, the shaded area goes through a color change. In essence, a specific area in which the shadow falls changes to a lower valued color, increasing its toned or shaded quality. Additionally, the coloration is most intense at the point of origin. As the shadow moves farther away from the object which causes the shaded area, the colors lighten and become blurred.

Often we think of black or gray when we want to create a shadow. But these hues leave a cold, flat appearance which looks unnatural. From Chevreul's discoveries and the experiments of the French Impressionists, we can see that using nature's clues works best.

Shadows can take on colors that surround them. The hues of a meadowland's wildflowers and grasses can mingle with a shadow's coloration. The colors of the sky can mix optically with the shadow colors. If the sky is blue, the shadow may have a blue cast; if it is lavender, then lavender may be incorporated in the colors. It is your decision whether to include these influences.

Figure 5-3 Shadows Change in Color, Intensity, Value, and Clarity

PRACTICAL GUIDELINE FOR CHOOSING SHADOW HUES

Try not to make your shadow just one color. If you do, the shadow will look flat and may not readily be perceived as a shadow. Instead, make your shadow a subtle mixture of closely blended hues and value changes.

Basically, a shaded area always moves in the direction of violet—toward the bottom of the color wheel. If you have a slightly shaded area, choose your color by moving one step down on the color wheel from the original color (photos 45, 46). A shadow cast on an orange design element could be made from red-orange. This new color could be either from the shade or the tone scale, depending on the value and intensity of the overall design. To shade a yellow-green, make the shadow from a color of lower value on the color wheel, such as green or blue-green. Again, it would be toned or shaded. See photo 1 for color wheel steps.

If your shadow is deep or quite dark, the shaded color may move many steps downward on the color wheel. Besides changing its hue, the shadow will also be grayed (toned) or blackened (shaded) to a greater extent than its original non-shadowed color (photos 22, 74).

VALUES IN DIFFERENT LIGHTING

The brighter the light source, the more intense the shadow will be. This results in a greater value change within the shadow. If the light source is soft and subtle, the shadow will be more subtle; the value changes will be limited. Sometimes when a design includes both shadows and highlights, the values of the different elements can be confusing. For example, if you have a dark rust triangle in intense light and a light apricot triangle in dark shadow, it may mean that the darkest colored triangle will appear to be the lightest.

Before creating shadows in your design, carefully think through the value changes, the possibilities for color play, and the perceptions you wish to create.

Highlights

In some designs you may wish to create the illusion of highlights. This effect happens in nature when light shines so intensely that it interferes with our ability to see clearly (photos 24, 40, 45). When the sun's strong rays prevent you from seeing distinctly as you walk through a sun-drenched forest, you are witnessing a form of highlighting. Since highlighting is the result of intense sunlight that evokes a warm feeling throughout the area, a tinge of warm pale yellow, cream, or pink is vaguely seen in most highlights.

When creating a highlight, do not make your most intense hues higher in value than the light source. Contrastingly, however, the value of the highlight does need to be higher than surrounding colors that are perceived to be in shade.

GUIDELINES FOR CHOOSING HIGHLIGHT HUES

For highlighting, the basic guidelines include moving your colors upward on the color wheel. Yellow is the highest valued color on the color wheel, so all highlighted colors move toward yellow (photos 1, 45, 46). If your highlighted area is already toned or shaded, it will not only become higher valued, but will become less toned or shaded. In other words, the highlight should be more pure than the original color. Do not use tints to create highlights from colors in the shade, pure, or tone scales; this would look unrealistic.

A highlighted toned turquoise object would move upward at least one step on the color wheel, to blue-green. The new color would also have less gray in it than the original hue. If the highlight is quite intense, the color can move several steps up on the color wheel, while increasing its purity. It may become a green or a yellow-green, depending on the brilliance of the highlight.

LIGHT, LANDSCAPES, AND TIME OF DAY

The quality of light changes constantly from the moment the sun begins to rise until the last shred of light disappears at night. If you want your landscape interpretations to look natural, whether abstract or realistic, be aware of the subtle color differences that occur during the day.

Morning hues are cool, tending toward delicate tints (photos 32, 80). By afternoon, the earth has warmed up and colors have become warmer under the sun's light. Late afternoon colors are stronger, warmer, and richer than in the morning. By evening, with the sun's glow apparent, colors are most often tinged with red and gold. Sometimes these evening hues can be very brilliant (photo 16).

Colors change as lighting changes. As light increases or decreases, changes also take place in colors and their value and intensity. As darkness draws upon us, colors begin to move downward toward the next lower hue on the color wheel. This movement continues downward as the lighting diminishes (photos 42, 81). Values become lower and intensity lessens. When light increases, color moves upward on the color wheel, one color at a time (photo 50). Additionally, values become higher, with hues becoming more intense.

When the moon rises, warm hues are often still present, giving off an appearance of reds, violets, and purples. Therefore, shadows from the moon may lean more toward purples during the early stages of the moon's rising. As the moon gains height, the light becomes more yellow. However, when the moon is high in the sky, the illumination changes to a bluish color. When this blueness intermingles with the green vegetation of trees, leaves, and grasses, moonlight tends to give it a silvery cast. Mist, which is moisture in the air, gives a mystical green cast to the landscape when mixed with yellowish moonlight. When creating a nighttime landscape entirely illuminated by moonlight, areas that do not capture the light of the moon in your picture will be almost entirely dark.

The Grande Dame of Light—The Auroras

Many beautiful phenomena in nature make excellent themes or focal points in art. These include sun and moon halos, mirages, ice crystals, and scintillating stars. The most glorious of all these natural phenomena are the aurora borealis and the aurora australis, the dancing lights of the Northern and Southern Hemispheres. If you have ever seen an aurora, you know the awe and wonder such an event inspires. Auroras are beautiful, wondrous displays of color in the sky.

The auroras are caused by huge explosive storms on the sun, known as flares. These sun explosions release small particles that become trapped in the magnetic field and are forced into Earth's upper atmosphere, where they collide with atoms. This collision causes electrons to separate from stricken atoms. Loose electrons are then picked up by other atoms. As the electrons attach themselves to other atoms, a flash of light energy results. The light from millions of electrons reuniting with atoms causes the glorious colors of the auroras.

Auroras can look like large arcs in the sky; they can serpentine; or they can appear like an enormous draping curtain. These last are the most dramatic and brightest auroras, with their exquisite, graceful motion and flowing colorations. They are often a greenish-white color. The lower edge of this type of aurora is quite sharply defined, while the upper portion is unclear. This type of aurora creates an aura, or corona, which looks like colors shooting upward from the bottom of the curtain.

Although auroras may be seen at different times of the day, they occur frequently near midnight. At dusk, their light may begin to appear very dimly. Over the next several hours the colors begin to blend, glowing and moving gracefully. They may start with a greenish yellow coloration that gradually blends into the pinks, reds, and purples. At the climax of the aurora the curtains move, folding and unfolding. The hues seem to quiver intensely, enveloping the entire sky. Then within a few minutes the colors begin to fade, until finally all that remains is a luminous glow of faint light.

Creating Auroras in Your Artwork

The possibilities of making a design using the aurora as the theme are limitless. Auroras lend themselves to abstract designs (photo 19), yet a realistic nightscape with the aurora flowing above could be breathtaking. Even a traditional quilt design of triangular or square shapes can be an excellent format for creating artwork with an aurora theme if the colors are strategically placed.

IRIDESCENCE AND OPALESCENCE

Some of the most beautiful hues in the world are created not by dyes or pigments, but by a natural process of interference. A fleeting rainbow, a bird's iridescence, and a gem's opalescence are all created by a type of interference that takes place as light waves react when they strike an object in their path that interferes with their movement.

Iridescence and opalescence are the most elusive and mysterious colors of all, glistening in a display of beautiful spectral hues with every movement. Some colorations are more intense than others. A rainbow is delicately iridescent, while the feathers of a strutting male peacock are the most vibrant of all. The beautiful array of colors in an Australian fire opal shimmers brilliantly with its tiny slits of spectral hues, while its distant relative, the lovely mother-of-pearl, lends itself to more obscure, soft colors. Both display a form of opalescence—a name given to objects that have the same characteristics as an opal—a milky, softer version of iridescence.

To use iridescence and opalescence in your art, it helps to understand how these two illusions come into existence in nature. Therefore, background information about the formation of iridescence and opalescence in nature is included here. Suggestions on how to incorporate these magical illusions are also presented.

Rainbows: A Display of Prismatic Interference

One of nature's best examples of iridescence is the rainbow. The magical, ever-fleeting appearance of a rainbow, a form of prismatic interference, makes it an especially intriguing theme for art.

When light waves pass through the atmosphere and strike rain droplets, water, or dust particles, the change in density from air to the interfering object causes the light waves to bend. The greater the difference between the density of air and the interfering mass, the more the waves bend. This bending is called *refraction*. A rainbow appears because light rays strike raindrops as they head toward earth. As the light rays are refracted, the water droplets act like individual prisms, separating the rays into bands of rainbow colors (figure 5-4).

Figure 5-4 The Rainbow

Rainbows always form in the same seven bands of color: red, orange, yellow, green, blue, indigo, and violet. Red is on the outside of the rainbow, and violet is on the inside. This order never changes. When the light waves break down into their rainbow colors (spectral colors), red rays bend the least; thus that color's outside position. Violet rays are bent most, resulting in their innermost placement. All colors between red and violet refract at angles between these two extremes, and appear in an order that reflects the angles of their refraction. Because light waves hit billions of raindrops at one time, refraction causes the rain to act like a giant prism in the sky.

Rainbows occur when sun and rain are simultaneously present in the sky. Not only do raindrops and sunlight have to co-exist, but the angle of the sun must be no more than 41 degrees above the horizon line. When the sun is higher in the sky, as at midday, the light-wave angle is too sharp to produce a rainbow. During a morning rainbow, the sun is at your back in the east and the rainbow is in the west. For an afternoon rainbow, the sun will be behind you, toward the west, with the rainbow in the east. Anyone who sees a rainbow is always positioned between the rainbow and the sun.

Making Iridescent Waves: Oil Slicks and Soap Bubbles

Some glorious iridescent colorations are formed by nature through a process called *constructive* and *destructive interference*. This type of iridescence relates to colors produced from filmy matter such as oil slicks and soap bubbles. Although it sounds complicated, constructive and destructive interference is similar to the wave action we see at a beach. Some waves look enormous far away, but as they come closer to shore, they seem to dissipate. At other times, very mellow waves suddenly become enormous, amplifying in size as they break close to shore. The majority of waves seem inconsequential, being rather weak or commonplace in strength and size. Not only do waves change size, but some waves pick up speed, while others slow down.

The exact same actions happen to light waves in the air. Both light and water waves have a high point called a crest and a low point called a trough (figure 5-5). When waves unite, sometimes their crests and troughs are identical in size and motion, so one wave action is added to the other, with their total size equaling the sum of both. This is called constructive interference (figure 5-6).

When two waves, water or air, meet where the trough of one unites with the crest of another, they seemingly cancel each other out. This is called destructive interference, as the size becomes the difference between the two (figure 5-7). However, if the two waves are not synchronized, so that their troughs and crests neither amplify nor nullify the wave size, the wave becomes inconsequential, or incidental. These three variations are called phases of the wave.

When light hits a puddle of water that has an oil film on it, the phases of the light waves dictate the colors seen and their strength. Some portion of the light waves reflects off the oil film immediately, while the remaining part of the waves continues their forward motion. Light waves cannot travel at the same speed in liquid as they do in air. So, having hit a surface that is denser than air, the waves slow down, bend, and continue their progress until they can go no farther, hitting the ground or some other surface.

Once the waves hit bottom (or the next interfering surface), they bend and begin the return trip back up through the film, where they meet their wave counterparts. If the two parts of the wave are in the exact same phase, the colors will be added together, resulting in brilliant, strong, pure hues. If the two are on opposite phases, no colors appear. When the two waves are slightly out of phase, they form weak colors.

Figure 5-5 Wave Action

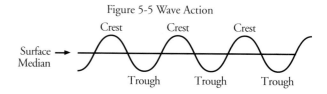

Figure 5-6 Constructive Interference
Both waves are identical, so waves are added together, becoming twice as large.

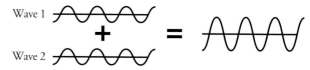

Figure 5-7 Destructive Interference
Both waves are in opposite phases; as one goes up the other goes down, cancelling each other out.

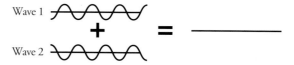

The colors we see in soap bubbles are created similarly, with the film of the bubble causing interference as the waves hit the surface. Some parts of the light waves continue on until they strike the other side of the bubble's thin skin; they then bounce back from this second surface, eventually reuniting with the other waves.

Every time a change takes place in the angle or the distance of a light wave's path, a different color appears. The interference either eliminates, dilutes, or strengthens iridescent colors, depending on the phases of the corresponding light waves and how much their waves have been amplified, when in phase.

FLEETINGLY BEAUTIFUL COLORS THROUGH DIFFRACTION

Some magnificently colored creatures acquire their coloration by a process called *structural interference.* These include hummingbirds, butterflies, beetles, and tropical fish. With this group, the light rays break apart and spread out into various hues as they hit the various parts of the creature's body. This spreading apart of light waves is called *diffraction.* Visually, there is no difference between the refractive (bending) colors of rainbows and those hues created through diffraction (figure 5-8).

Diffraction also occurs when light rays attempt to pass through small openings called *diffraction gratings.* In nature, these minute gratings are so close together that an entire light ray cannot pass through unscathed and is deflected. The ray then breaks apart and scatters the wave into visible rainbow hues. Colors are weakened, eliminated, or strengthened by the position of the waves in their different phases. The coloration of the hues is intensified further by movement, either of the object or of the viewer. The metallic iridescent hues of certain birds and insects are produced by the diffraction of light as it hits millions of tiny holes (diffraction gratings) in feathers and other body parts. Mother-of-pearl in mollusk shells is created similarly.

THE CREATION OF AN OPAL

An opal may be one of the most familiar objects that obtains its hues by diffraction. Opals are formed deep in

Figure 5-8 Structural Iridescence

Figure 5-9 The Peacock's Glory: Space Latticing

the earth where dissolved silica is trapped in pools of water. Eventually the water evaporates and the silica molecules attach to each other, forming small spheres. As time passes, these silica spheres begin to bond tightly together by layers. When the water evaporates, the layers harden, leaving spaces where water once was. When light hits these voids, it causes the waves to either diffract (spread out) or become absorbed.

As an opal moves, or as the viewer turns, the patterns and depth in the spaces change slightly, causing the colors to change. This creates the effect of the colors coming from deep within the stone; thus the name fire opal. The stacks of spheres in the fire opal resemble a diffraction grate. Therefore, when the light rays hit these tiny openings, the waves break apart, spreading out into the rainbow colors (photo 49).

An opal made up of small spheres and spaces generally exhibits violet and blue lights, or those with the shortest wavelengths. Opals that have larger spheres and spaces usually include the full spectrum of rainbow colors (photo 51). Opals with multi-layered spheres are much more brilliantly colored than those with spheres that lack either multiple layers or structured order.

THE PROUDLY STRUTTING PEACOCK: SPACE LATTICE INTERFERENCE

The most exquisite coloring in the world is due to a type of interference called *space lattice interference.* It incorporates the most intricate type of diffraction grating known to man. This submicroscopic structure, called the space lattice, cannot be seen by the naked eye. It is made up of minute layers of lattice that have tiny openings evenly spaced so that light plays finely on the different elements in the structure. The precision of the minuscule structures that create these beautiful plays of color is currently impossible for man to duplicate.

The only creature we are aware of that has this type of structural coloring is the male peacock (figure 5-9). Although there is no actual coloring in his feathers, intense colors appear due to light waves being reflected, refracted, and diffracted through this intricate submicroscopic multi-layered lattice in the peacock's feathers.

In space latticing, a portion of the light waves is diffracted and reflected from the top layer immediately upon hitting the feather structure. Another part of the light waves is refracted and reflected into the grated layers directly underneath. Then, the remainder goes deep within the lower regions of the space lattice, also being refracted and reflected.

The space lattice is a finely tuned instrument that has been designed so that the spectral colors of the various light waves amplify greatly because they coincide in their wave phases. The more layers of lattice there are within the structure, the more pure and intense the colors become. Colors created by space latticing are the most brilliant, pure colors in the world. If the space lattice of a peacock is destroyed or crushed, the body coloring disappears, and the creature becomes a colorless gray.

Using Iridescence in Your Art

To obtain iridescence or opalescence in your art, work with the same colors that create rainbows, beautiful fleeting colorations in opals, the shimmering hues of tropical fish and butterflies, or the stunning pure colors of peacock feathers.

As a general rule, use strong, intense pure colors set against black or deep, dark shades to attain iridescence. Eggplant, purple, dark teal, or deep forest green are excellent choices to set against the jewel tones of iridescence. The choice depends on your artistic theme. The colors of the grand peacock in all his splendorous intensity can be exquisite with the darkest versions of shades as background (photos 44, 65).

For opalescence, use sparkling tints with a toned background. The soft subtle colorations of opalescence are more aptly teamed with a hue that provides a grayed, milky look. This can be a creamy white or gray, or even a high-valued grayed lavender (photos 49, 51).

In your design, place colors spontaneously so they dance across the surface in an unplanned manner. A formal color pattern usually does not work when you are attempting to create iridescence. A structured design with defined color placement is probably not the best choice to elicit iridescence or opalescence; an asymmetrical or abstract design is most suitable for this type of coloration. Exceptions, of course, can be made.

If you look at iridescent tropical fish, you will notice that the entire range of color schemes is represented. These fish show: (1) monochromatic colors such as blues, ranging from pale blue to a dark royal; (2) analogous hues

of yellow, green, and turquoise or even yellow, orange, and coral; (3) complementary partnerships such as magenta and green; (4) split-complementary combinations of sparkling yellow-orange, yellow, yellow-green and violet; or (5) triadic hues with vivid yellow-green, blue, and red.

Butterflies are often seen in the analogous, complementary, and split-complementary color schemes. It is not unusual to see a butterfly with hues of blue and yellow-orange or a range of reds and oranges with a blue accent.

As for the opalescence of precious stones, the tints are often analogous, such as green, blue-green, and blue. Sometimes hints of complementary colors are interspersed, resulting in a split-complementary color scheme with some intermingling of colors.

When you create your own design using iridescence or opalescence, plan to follow nature as much as possible. Before starting your creation, study pictures of tropical fish, butterflies, precious gems, and birds—most particularly birds of paradise, pheasants, and peacocks. These observations will give you a feel for the hues, their fleeting qualities, and the most prevalent color combinations. It is very difficult to create a realistic representation of iridescence or opalescence unless you familiarize yourself with the colors and their elusive effects. For suggestions on how to enhance the quality of iridescence and opalescence in fabric, see Chapter 7, page 55.

Besides considering the color scheme to use, remember that the colors in the design will change in hue and value. This change represents movement or the shifting of hues as movement seems to take place. Iridescent colors are strongly intense, being the most pure of all colors. The changes may range from the highest key or middle key to the lowest key in value. Depending on your theme, the colors you choose can range from the most brilliant hues possible to the most subtle.

Whenever your design represents curving, folding, or overlapping colors that shift the hues away from the viewer, they should deepen. These crevasses of color definition are often created in analogously shaded hues, falling into the deepest blends of the hues represented.

Part of the beauty and vibrance of iridescence is the shifting of high- and medium-valued colors placed against low-valued hues. The contrasts are often great, yet because of the shades used, they are rich and harmonious rather than distracting. Iridescence is a wonderful illusion to create when you want a bold, exciting design that exhibits spontaneity. Opalescence is perfect for subtle designs using fleeting, high-valued colors.

CHAPTER 6

More Illusions To Tease the Mind

Some of the most fascinating illusions to pique our imagination are introduced in this chapter. These illusions are not particularly related, yet are bound together by the fact that they include some of the illusions most desired in art. Movement through color and mist are wondrously elusive artistic fantasies. Reflections capture our awe as we see the mirrored image of a form lying before us. Transparency has always intrigued artists and laymen alike because of its wonderful color play. Three-dimensionality, or depth, is an effect often desired in art. So, if you wish to create magical, fleeting imageries, have a great time exploring these wonderful illusions.

DEPTH

Visual art on a flat surface has only two dimensions, width and length. When we want to present depth on this surface, we add a third dimension. This additional dimension is called *perspective*. *Aerial perspective* is used for most landscape pictures. However, when you create buildings, roads, or other manmade structures in art, you may choose *linear perspective*. When you work with cubes and other forms of volume, linear perspective or a combination of both systems may be your choice.

Aerial Perspective

Leonardo da Vinci, a Florentine artist and engineer, is given credit for developing aerial perspective. This form of perspective is achieved primarily by changing color values and intensities in the artwork as objects recede into the distance. Land formations and objects also diminish in size as they recede. Aerial perspective is also called atmospheric perspective, color perspective, visual depth, and depth.

BASIC PRINCIPLES OF AERIAL PERSPECTIVE

Aerial perspective, or visual depth, is achieved by elements in a design becoming lighter, grayer, and more blurred as they recede into the distance. Any textural scale or details should also diminish in size and clarity as the elements move toward the background. Additionally, as the formations recede, their sizes change, becoming smaller as they move farther into the background (figure 6-1; photos 16, 18, 22, 28, 32, 50).

Figure 6-1 Aerial Perspective, Visual Depth, Atmospheric Perspective
To achieve visual depth, as each land form recedes into the background, it becomes lighter, grayer, and less distinct than the one placed before it. The farther apart two land formations are, the greater the contrast of their color value.

THE FOREGROUND

Foreground colors should be the brightest, clearest, and most intense hues in your art (photos 22, 36). If there is a temperature contrast in your land elements, the foreground colors should be the warmest (photo 31).

Your foreground colors can be related or unrelated to the rest of the picture. For instance, you may create a picture of a view from your summer flower garden looking out toward meadows and hills beyond. The garden may be splashed with yellows, blues, oranges, violets, and other dynamic colors, while your background features may be made from a completely different set of hues. If you want to develop a feeling of continuity between the different elements in your picture, relate your foreground colors to the middle-distant and background hues (photos 28, 31, 35, 73).

THE MIDDLE DISTANCES

The elements of design in the middle distance will be somewhat smaller than those in the foreground. If you have trees or other objects in both the foreground and middle areas, those in the middle distance will always appear smaller in size, even if they are the same height in actuality. This change in size will always promote the visual illusion of depth (photos 16, 32). Middle-distance colors will be lighter in value, lower in intensity (grayer), cooler in temperature (bluer), and less distinct in texture and detail (more blurred) than foreground colors (photo 36).

Particles in the air obscure our vision so that distant elements are not as clear as those nearby. This haze brought on by vapor, dust, and other airborne particles increases with distance. Therefore, the farther distanced a land formation is, the more hazy and toned it becomes. Consequently, if you want to duplicate the effects of nature, you must gray and cool the hues of the background more than the middle-distance colors.

Besides graying, distinct details and textures of the landscape blur in the distance. Details all but evaporate in the most distant hills or mountains (photo 31). This same background elusiveness should be duplicated in non-landscape art that includes three-dimensionality. To show contrast between the background and the focal point, the background should be grayed, muted, blurred, or nondistinct (photos 27, 43, 58, 63, 78).

PERCEPTION OF DISTANCE BETWEEN LAND FORMATIONS

When you look into the distance, notice that the farther apart two land formations are, the greater the contrast in color value and intensity (photos 74, 80). Make the value and intensity contrasts pronounced if you want to show land formations that are far in the distance (photo 36). When you want to give the perception of proximity, the value change should be slight (photos 16, 73). The same is true for abstract and geometric designs. The different value and intensity contrasts visually define the relationship between the design elements (photos 46, 56, 58, 78, 82, 83).

ADDITIONAL WAYS TO ACCENTUATE DISTANCE

You can create a feeling of distance by overlapping land formations, structures, or other abstract shapes in your picture. For examples of art expressing depth through overlapping, see photos 20, 23, 24, 42, 51, 53, 54, 63, 75, 76, and 83. Even when the visual image is expressed abstractly, the overlapping and grayness of background gives a feeling of depth. The interplay of values with the darkest forms advancing while the subdued toned hues recede into the distance can give the gentle impression of depth (photos 35, 49).

LINEAR PERSPECTIVE

Linear perspective is particularly useful when you need precision in your design. Also, in a landscape, you may have a structure such as a house. This can easily be done with linear perspective. Instructions for using linear perspective are included in Appendix I. For art using linear perspective, see photos 27, 45, and 58.

Color and Space—Volume and Form

The most important aspect of space, volume, and form is the element of contrast. For effective use of color, it is important to contrast the temperature, intensity, and values of the various hues. Along with these contrasts, be mindful of where you want your design to recede and advance. Make your color placements accordingly. To promote visual depth, contrasts are used to accentuate the differences between the background and the foreground. However, if the contrasts are only subtly different, each competes with the other, and depth decreases strongly.

If you contrast a high-valued element (yellow) with a low-valued element in the same plane (purple), the highest-valued form appears closer. Likewise, if you make a contrast between two elements that are warm or cool in hue, the warm color advances (photos 17, 21, 24, 25, 30, 33, 42, 43). Colors that are more pure or intense than another tend to advance (photos 58, 66, 68).

Designs with bright, pure colors of both warm and cool temperatures express depth. Using the same colors, but toning them considerably, diminishes depth. If you take the same two colors and gray one but not the other, you will find that the toned hue recedes in contrast to the pure color.

In some designs, you can add volume by creating the effect of light hitting an object. In designs using forms, volume can be accentuated by having light on one side and shadows on another (photos 45, 46). See Chapter 5, pages 38 to 40 for information on how to create shadows and highlights.

ACHIEVING FLATNESS

If you want to accentuate the illusion of flatness in your design, consider using hues of the same color temperature. This tends to nullify the advance of one color over the other. If you want to use hues of contrasting temperature, the color values and intensity need to be similar. To further the flatness, minimize all contrasts as much as possible.

UNDERWATER PERSPECTIVE

Our vision is limited in both distance and clarity underwater, primarily because light waves have a more difficult time passing through water. Water's density also deflects light waves; thus we get distortions under water. Also, many of the light waves become scattered in the water, so light is fairly ineffectual. Our ability to see depends on the depth of water, how much light passes into the water, the time of day, and how many particles are present in the water.

You can create a much more realistic underwater scene when your formations are blurred, with soft, undefined edges. Because distortion is created by the slowing and bending of the light rays, most objects look fractured. Color, design, and textures should be perceived as ambiguous or obscure to add realism. When

Figure 6-2 Reflections
Generally, a reflection is the same height as the object being reflected. Reflections do not curve; they are vertically positioned in front of the viewer.

water colors are deep, and figures are shadowy, shades and low-valued tones are excellent colors. When the water is clear and light, as in the Caribbean, the figures can be bright, clear, and covered with detail because the visibility illusion is much greater. Tints and pure colors would be perfect for figures in this situation. The distortion factor is still prevalent, however.

REFLECTIONS IN THE LANDSCAPE

A reflection often enhances a landscape picture, but its use is not restricted to purely representational art. It is generally used to mirror the area of central focus. It usually repeats the form, size, and color of this element. Reflections are easy to create when nature's guidelines are followed. For an example of reflection, see figure 6-2.

Height

A reflection is the same height as the element that is being reflected. Thus, if a grove of trees extends twelve inches above the water line in a picture, the reflection must extend twelve inches into the water. The notable exceptions to this rule are the reflections of the sun and moon on water or land.

Positioning

Reflections extend vertically; they do not angle or curve. Even if you walk to the left or right twenty paces, the reflection will still be in a straight line and vertically positioned in front of you (photos 22, 38).

Colors and Values of Reflections

A reflection often takes on the colors of the object being reflected. The reflection can be lighter, darker, or even the same value. If the elements being reflected are high valued and intense, the reflection will be more brilliant and airy (photo 37) than reflections of darkly col-

ored objects (photos 22, 77). Darker elements will cast deeper colored reflections (photo 38).

The sky and water colors, along with the location of the sun in the sky, also influence the coloring of a reflection. When the sun is setting behind hills, the reflection of those hills on the water can be very dark—almost like a silhouette of the hills. When the sun is high in the sky, the colors can be lighter or identical in value. If the water has its own powerful coloration, it can play a dominant role in the reflected element's coloring. When this happens, the colors can mingle or take on a darker, deeper version of the water coloring.

Movement Within a Reflection

Water movement also has a bearing on reflections in water. If the water is without a ripple, the reflection will be a perfect mirrored image (photo 22). If there is a small amount of movement in the water, then the reflection blurs slightly (photo 38). This can also lighten the reflection. When the water is choppy, the reflection becomes distorted, resulting in an impressionistic effect (photo 37). Rain and wind both cause disturbed water, which can lead to a distorted or impressionistic reflection (photo 77).

Reflections of the Sun and Moon

The size of the sun's or moon's reflection on water is determined primarily by the height of the sun or moon in the sky. Weather and wave action can also affect the size. When the sun or moon is high in the sky, the reflection is shorter and wider than when either is lower. As the sun or moon moves toward the horizon line, the reflection becomes long and narrow. When either the sun or moon sits just above the horizon line, the reflection is simply a narrow column of color spanning across the water (figure 6-3). The brightest part of the

Figure 6-3 A Reflection of the Sun or Moon
The lower the sun or moon is in the sky, the longer and narrower the reflection is on the water. The higher the sun and moon are in the sky, the wider and shorter the reflection. The reflection is most intense closest to the horizon.

reflection begins near the horizon. It softens and lightens in value as it skips across the water.

Objects in the Water

If you see a boat or any other object on the water, it will appear as if a mirror was placed at the waterline, as the reflection will include part of the object's underside. If the water is still, the reflection will be perfectly mirrored. Any wave action in the water distorts the reflection (figure 6-4). When the water appears choppy, only the impression of the shape and color will reflect onto the water.

Mingling Colors in a Reflection

With some objects, it's difficult to determine how to create the reflection. Try to observe the object, the light, and the surface on which the reflection is made. Photographs of reflections that particularly interest you are very helpful, especially if you make a study of the reflection during different times of the day. It is not necessary to create exact reflections of an object. Instead, you may create the impression of a reflection. This can be done through an impressionistic display of color, value, intensity, and form that gives the perception of a reflection.

When the reflection falls on a glossy surface, the reflected area can be bright. Also, its edges will be sharply defined. Many details may show. However, if the surface is dull, the reflection will be rather ambiguous, resulting only in a perception of a reflection. This is done through changes in color, value, intensity, and abstract form. The shape of the reflection will be unclear, undefined, and without details.

Reflected colors in folded or draped objects, such as flower petals, interact uniquely. Wherever the fold or draping occurs, colors vary slightly and take on greater intensity. This hue variation may actually lean toward one of the adjacent colors. This intensity increase and color change happens as a result of multiple reflections. Whenever multiple reflections occur, the colors interact, mingle, and change, becoming stronger and slightly varied.

Echoing of colors that reflect one on another happens quite readily in nature, especially in flowers. We observe this illusion every day, but rarely analyze the colors. For instance, we can see colors echoing when the reflections of two metallic Christmas ornaments on a tree reflect on each other. If light shines on blue and pink metal balls hanging close to each other, each color reflects on the other. The result is an interesting blend of colors which echo each other's characteristics.

Figure 6-4 A Reflection of an Object in Water

TRANSPARENCY

Transparency is one of the most delightful illusions to create. Because there are three types of transparency, their effects in a design can be quite varied. Each form of transparency gives a slightly different impression: (1) both colors appear transparent at their point of intersection, so that it seems you can look through both hues and see the area beyond; (2) the top color appears to be a film lying on an opaque bottom color at their point of intersection; (3) one color appears to float above the other. You can use each of these forms of transparency independently, or include them all in the same art. If you wish to create a transparency effect, you must make it look as though the bottom color exists and can be seen slightly, due to the top color's transparency. For examples of transparency, see photos 41, 47, 53, 62, 85, and 86.

With paints, transparency is achieved by mixing two colors together to form a third color. The two original colors are the parent colors, and the hue created by mixing them is the offspring, or hybrid, color.

Creating the Offspring of Two Transparent Parents

When two parent colors are thoroughly mixed in even proportions, the offspring color becomes the middle hue and value of the two parent colors. If parent colors are similar in their receding and advancing qualities, and are fairly similar in value, their offspring color will give the illusion of both colors being transparent (photo 13A). If you combine a high-valued golden yellow with a high-valued lime-green, the offspring color will be a high-valued yellowish-green. Because this new hue is the midpoint in value and hue of the two parent colors, the effect is a transparency that seems to be backlit.

A similar effect happens if you make a bow of green and yellow cellophane. Each bow drapes with its own coloration when set alone, but wherever the two colors cross paths, they not only combine to form a new color, but you can see through the two pieces of cellophane into the distant background.

Creating the Offspring of
Transparent and Opaque Parent Colors

When the offspring color is not equally distant between the two parent colors in value or hue, the hybrid hue most resembles the parent color it leans closest to. In this form of transparency, one color appears transparent while the other is opaque. In essence, the top color acts like a thin transparent film lying over the second, opaque color (photo 13B with a yellow film over the blue; photo 13C with a blue film over the yellow).

In a yellow and turquoise design, the offspring may be a yellow-green. This, then, will appear closest to the yellow parent. In the design, the yellow will appear to be on top of the turquoise. If the offspring color is a blue-green, it will be more aligned with the turquoise color. When this happens, the turquoise will appear to be on top.

Floating Transparent Colors

If two parent colors are highly contrasted in hue, value, and temperature, there is a good possibility that one color will seem to float on top of the other color. The visual space between the two colors can appear close or far apart. This spatial difference depends on the parent colors, their characteristics, and the mixed color chosen as the offspring (photo 13D with light apricot over a navy blue; photo 13E with navy blue over light apricot).

COLOR MOVEMENT

If you analyze a photograph of a moving object, you will see areas of clarity and blurring. Most often the moving object is blurred, while the background is quite clear. This, in fact, depicts the most accentuated motion (figure 6-5). However, if the photographer has panned the picture so that the camera moves along with the moving object, the background will be blurred, giving only an impression of the background (figure 6-6).

Figure 6-6 Achieving Motion with a Blurred Background

If you watch a spinning top, you do not see its edges clearly because of the movement. The colors fade into a blend, mixing together in horizontal, diagonal, or vertical streaks, depending on the original design. These streaks of color seem to go beyond the actual form, making it impossible to see the edges clearly (figure 6-5).

Motion can be emphasized by not quite completing the focal design. Make the object fade in and out of focus. It is sometimes blurred, sometimes clearly defined, and sometimes a mixture of the two (photo 53). When you blur your design, remember that a blur has no defined edges or corners. Everything appears to fade away.

The suggestion of motion can be accentuated by extending the form's edges vaguely into the background. This can be done through a certain amount of abstraction. You can also make the values of the object and background change in contrast. Sometimes the values will contrast highly so that the edges are quite defined, while at other times the values are so close that the edges and background seem to merge. This juggling of values between the background and object's edges creates the feeling of movement.

When motion is desired, details are taken away. The images are simply suggestions of what your mind may recognize, rather than a clear definition. It is also important to note that patterns of light and dark values of color placed sporadically in the design help elicit a feeling of motion.

Fluidity and rhythmic repetition in both color and design increase the illusion of motion in a work of art. To accentuate this movement, it is important to duplicate movement's quickness and fluidity. This is most easily done by moving color abstractly through your entire design field (photo 19). See the rain movement and water movement in photo 77.

Figure 6-5 Achieving Motion with a Blurred Object

Additional Suggestions for Creating Motion

You can create a sense of motion by moving from one extreme in shape or color to another. For instance, moving a design from light colors through dark colors, or dark colors to light, enhances movement. Or, you can change shapes throughout your design from small to large (photo 28). Again, these can be enhanced through abstraction in the design changes.

Linear Movement

Generally, a straight line gives a static effect in a design unless it is purposefully broken up to suggest movement. In contrast, a curved line almost always promotes the illusion of motion. However, by altering straight lines, you can make a straight line seem to have movement. For instance, a scintillating star's straight lines appear to flicker and move because the lines are broken and slightly offset. For art that elicits the feeling of movement by breaking up lines, see photo 23.

MIST AND ATMOSPHERIC COLOR

In mist, you cannot see very far into the distance. Everything is subdued, blurred, and very toned in mist. Often the colors in the field fade in and out of vision with no particular pattern. Mist adds a film to the colors beyond it. If trees are behind mist, the colors that show through are their green hues. For an example of mist, see figure 6-7.

Figure 6-7 Mist

As an artist, you can veil mist in any color you wish, remembering that everything is in relatively high-valued tones. Distinct details, forms, and lines would be unusual in misty conditions. Design elements are sporadically visible. Colors vacillate in strength by shifting values. Mist is often created through gentle gradations of high-valued toned hues (photo 26).

"Form is based, first, upon a supposition, a theme. Form is, second, a marshaling of materials, the inert matter in which theme is to be cast. Form is, third, a setting of boundaries, of limits, the whole extent of idea, but no more, an outer shape of idea. Form is, next, the relating of inner shapes to the outer limits, the initial establishing of harmonies. Form is, further, the abolishing of excessive content, of content that falls outside the true limits of the theme. It is the abolishing of excessive materials, whatever material is extraneous to inner harmony, to the order of shapes now established. Form is thus a discipline, an ordering according to the needs of content."

—Ben Shahn
American painter, 1898–1969
The Shape of Content

"Work madly and freely and you will make progress. Above all, don't labor over your picture. A great emotion can be translated immediately. Dream over it and look for the simplest form."

—Paul Gauguin
French painter, 1848–1903
The Impressionists

CHAPTER 7

Blending Fabric and Design Harmoniously

Fabric choice is of the utmost importance to design for a quilter or textile artist. When you make color choices you are like a painter, using the array of fabrics that surrounds you as your palette. When making choices, remember that fabric performs a dual role by bringing into play not only hues, but textural effects, similar to the way a painter uses a palette knife or other tool to achieve texture. Look at fabric, then, not only to provide a hue, but also as an intricate design feature that can further enhance art.

To have a vision and then transpose that imagery into available fabrics usually means constant compromises and adjustments. It also takes thought, patience, technical skill, and some luck to create the effects you desire. Using a fabric creatively in unexpected ways rather than for obvious choices can be both energizing and exciting.

Our fabric choices are much greater today than in preceding decades. Our options have increased so much that there is no reason to compromise design beauty with fabrics that are incompatible with our visual goals. Now we can buy from a wide spectrum of fabric choices including solids, calicos, geometric designs, painterly prints, whimsical colorations, and beautifully sophisticated designs. Designer fabrics, wild jungle prints, custom-dyed fabrics, and zany motifs can also be found in the selections for our medium. Decisions about which fabrics to use depend chiefly on the theme of our art, the specific design elements included, the mood we wish to evoke, the colors we wish to include, and our personal preferences.

Keeping a wide variety of fabric design styles available makes it easier to create beautiful surface designs. On the other hand, because there are so many choices to make, the selection process can become very complicated. With greater options, guidelines are less definitive and sometimes even ambiguous. This chapter, then, provides you with a wide array of information to help you make the best possible fabric selections for your creative adventures.

PURCHASING FABRIC TO MAKE GREAT QUILTS

In the market today, we find fabrics that incorporate many hues in a large-design repeat. We can buy these fabrics for their painterly effects rather than their total design. They often repeat the design every 12 to 24 inches rather than ½ inch to 2 inches as in most calico prints. The fabrics are very versatile and work beautifully in designs as a color palette source because they generally have wonderful gradations of color that create great painterly effects.

When buying these types of prints, concentrate on the colors in the pattern. Often you use only a small portion of a color gradation for any one work of art; rarely would you use the entire design. It is difficult to blend calicos with these painterly fabrics because they contain two completely different design styles. If you choose to mix them, do so with care.

Buying Tint Fabrics

Beautiful, soft tint fabrics are one of the key ingredients to many powerful illusions. The best time to look for tints is when fabrics for spring sewing are available. Build a collection of tint fabrics to have on hand when the need arises. If you search for a specific tint in the middle of winter, you will probably be disappointed. Consider buying at least ⅓ yard of each tint you can find. Then you will be able to create quilts with wonderful illusions throughout the year.

When purchasing hand-dyed fabrics, be aware that the only true tints are those created from bleached fabric. Unbleached fabric gives a tonal cast to the color, causing a grayed or yellowed, veiled look instead of a clear, sparkling effect. These light-colored fabrics are not tints, and cannot perform successfully as a tint requirement for certain color illusions.

An Innovative Way To Buy Fabrics

Consider buying fabric without regard to any particular project. Instead, select fabrics by what appeals to you at the moment. Generally, you will find yourself drawn to different fabrics on each shopping trip. Sometimes this results in the purchase of autumnal fabrics; at other times you may find your interest piqued by soft, subtle, wintery ones. You may be surprised at the selections your intuitive self makes, as the choices often seem contrary to your current projects or interests. However, sometime in the distant future you will feel a strong urge to create a design using many of the fabrics you have collected intuitively.

This inner selection process seems to know far in advance what art you will do in the future. If you have built your fabric collection by consistently buying what suits your fancy each time you visit a fabric store, more than likely you will already have your palette of fabrics in your own cupboards when you are ready to begin a new design.

If you follow your intuitive desires rather than attempting to buy everything for a project all at once, you often find that your art is more alive and responsive—and better reflects your inner spirit. When working in this manner, you may also find your creative spirit very much in tune with either the seasons of the year or other themes that are subconsciously important to you.

USING A LARGE VARIETY OF FABRIC DESIGNS

Selecting the appropriate fabric is of utmost importance when you are creating a surface design for a quilt or other textile art. Prints add an additional element of intrigue to your quilt. Although prints often enhance design, they also complicate the artist's creative decisions. Choose patterned fabrics carefully. Stay away from inappropriate, distracting patterns and colorations. Prints are not needed in all designs, but when you include them, enjoy the decision-making process.

A large variety of fabrics in your art is usually more visually appealing than just a few selections. In a traditional quilt, increase your fabric choices so that no two blocks use exactly the same fabrics. If possible, use dozens of different fabrics in your design. Choose fabrics that can be interchanged and that relate well to each other in hue and mood. When you include many fabrics, subtle changes cause the hues to vibrate against each other, intensifying their beauty and making a more interesting visual statement (photos 19, 30, 42, 44). When you use a large variety of fabrics in this manner, you need not worry about running out of any one fabric. Simply add new fabrics to your design as you find them. This gives you the option of using small amounts of each fabric, perhaps in ¼ to ½ yard amounts.

Also, when creating a quilt or textile art, try to use more than one fabric for the background. This increases the textural effect and enhances mingling of hues. Consequently, your design will be more interesting. It would not be unusual to use ten to fifteen fabrics from the same color family, if you had them available, rather than only one (photos 42, 63, 65). These fabrics can differ subtly in design, value, and intensity, thereby amplifying color interaction.

Working in this manner is fun because fabric placement options are limitless. You can explore color and fabric combinations, trying a variety of intriguing possi-

Figure 7-1 Varying the Scales of Print Fabrics
For optimum visual beauty, vary the scale of print fabrics adjacent to each other in your design.

bilities. Even putting the blocks together is exciting, because unexpected designs come into play. The entire process comes alive creatively, challenging you until the end. I invite you to work in this manner when creating both traditional and contemporary quilts.

When choosing fabrics, combine a variety of materials that result in harmonious design and color application. Generally speaking, fabrics should form a unified statement. Unless you intend it, no fabric should stand out conspicuously from the rest. Unintentionally allowing this detracts from your visual statement. As you continue to work toward visual unity in your designs, you will make wiser fabric choices.

Always try to make the best fabric selection possible for the visual statement you want to convey. If you feel uncomfortable about a particular fabric, go with your intuition and don't use it in your artwork.

Using Solid Colored Fabrics (Solids)

If you choose solid colored fabrics, use them wisely, allowing nature to be your guide. Notice that almost nothing in nature is made from only one color. Tree leaves intermingle with light to reflect many hues. This is also true of tree bark, flowers, hillsides, gardens, and any other areas we look at. This blending or mixing of hues creates depth, interest, and excitement between various color elements.

Large areas of one solid fabric produce a flatness that can be visually disappointing. It rarely gives the effect you want. If, instead, you create your own fabric in the same area by incorporating several fabrics as one, you will imitate nature's practice effectively (photos 31, 36, 50, 60, 82, 85).

WORKING WITH CALICOS AND SIMILAR PRINTS

Well-chosen fabrics add interest and texture to your designs, amplifying their beauty. However, many prints are inappropriate for certain designs. Knowing which prints to use and realizing the limitations of others gives you a creative advantage. Since calicos and other small prints are still a major part of the quiltmaker's printed fabric collection, guidelines for their use are included here. Be aware of the important characteristics of these prints to make the wisest possible fabric choices.

Scale

Generally, fabrics work best together when they vary in scale. Scale is the term used to compare the relative size of one print design to another. The size relationship can change as fabrics are intermixed. Whenever possible, include large-scaled, medium-scaled, and small-scaled prints in your quilts (figure 7-1).

What may be a medium-scaled print in one group of fabrics can be large-scaled in another collection, and small-scaled in yet another. When fabric designs of the same scale are placed side by side, their designs bleed visually into one another. With calico prints this usually presents a busy, distracting look (figure 7-2). It is best to vary the print scale unless you are keeping your scales similar for a specific design reason. For instance, traditional scrap quilts can be very successful when created with no regard to scale. The busyness of like-scaled fabrics evokes a charmingly quaint quality in this type of quilt (photos 43, 55).

Each of us has our own scale size preference. In your fabric collection, you will see a preponderance of one scale over the others. When you realize this, you can be conscious of this tendency when buying fabrics. Initially, it may be difficult to buy prints in a scale that feels uncomfortable to you. However, once you begin using varied scales with relative ease, you will notice that intermingling fabric scales intensifies and enhances your design.

Figure 7-2 Similar Scales Cause Busyness
When print scales are the same, the designs bleed into each other, causing a busy look.

Figure 7-3 Dominant Prints
Strong dominant print designs such as these do not blend well with other print fabrics.

Varying the Pattern

Along with scale, it is important to vary the design elements in various calico fabrics. All floral motifs, all geometric prints, or all pin dots causes too much repetition; this invites monotony. So incorporate as many different types of designs into your quilt as fabric choices and design elements will allow.

If you must include several fabrics of similar patterns or images, arrange them so that they are not adjacent to each other. A variety of patterns increases your quilt's interest and beauty. As with scale, you may find you prefer a certain type of pattern. As long as you know this you can monitor your buying habits to ensure a varied assortment of patterns to choose from when creating your quilts.

PROBLEM PRINT FABRICS

Even though you acquire many beautiful fabrics over the years, you may find some fabrics in your collection have obvious design or color problems. There are few good reasons to use poorly designed fabrics or busy prints in your quilts. Although there may be an appropriate time to use these fabrics to fit a specific need, it is generally wise to stay away from problem-plagued fabrics. They only detract from the overall artistic statement you so carefully conceived.

Do you have fabrics in your collection which never fit your projects? Are there fabrics you have had for years and never found a place for? If so, these fabrics probably contain design or color problems. Take out several of these fabrics and analyze their characteristics. Check to see if they fit into any of the following problem fabric groups.

Dominant Prints

Certain prints cause problems because they do not blend well with other fabrics. Checks, stripes, and large static geometric designs, paisleys, and strongly sophisticated marbled fabrics, for example, tend to pull out of a design (figure 7-3). Because of their visual dominance

Figure 7-4 Color Dominance in Prints
Print fabric should always have a dominant color.
Print designs in which colors compete for dominance,
such as the one above, are visually distracting.

over other prints, they are rarely harmonious. If you use any of these in your work, be aware of their limitations and the possible design complications they may impose. Your goal is to make a visually successful surface design. Include these difficult fabrics only when they impart a particular image you wish to evoke.

Prints with Too Many Colors

If you use calico fabrics, it is best to choose those that include only one or two color families. This results in a workable, harmonious effect. A calico's design beauty is created by variety in color value and intensity, rather than in the number of different colors. For best results, avoid designs that include incongruous color placement. Exceptions can be made, of course, if you want a busy look, or if a multicolored fabric is exactly what you need to achieve a certain illusion.

No Color Dominance

Fabric patterns should follow good design rules. Fabric designs with no dominant color ignore basic design principles. When two colors, or color families, compete for dominance, the viewer's gaze bounces back and forth between the hues, causing distraction and discomfort. Avoid fabrics with these design problems, because they can destroy your visual statement (figure 7-4). Instead, choose fabrics that include a clearly recognizable dominant color.

Stark White and High Contrasting Prints

White is the natural neutral in artwork using the tint scale. Because all tints are made from white, this is a natural partnership. Therefore, using an off-white with tints can deaden the art.

In other situations, however, stark white fabrics, like problem prints, can be distracting unless used carefully, because their strength can decrease your artwork's unity

by pulling out visually. Before using pure white, ask yourself if an off-white or other neutral might work better. A blush white—white with just a tinge of color in it—is often a good substitute. If you use white without a specific purpose in mind, include it cautiously. But when white helps you obtain your design objectives, use it.

Highly contrasting hues in the same print can also be distracting. For example, a white and navy blue fabric may look wonderful alone, but may detract from your total design (figure 7-5). In a Log Cabin design, a fabric with highly contrasting hues would be too dark for the white side and too light for the blue side. Although the colors may be compatible with the quilt, the fabric itself would not be. In most situations, these fabrics affect the work negatively because their visual contrast detracts from the artistic unity. Be aware of these fabrics and use them wisely.

Assessing Your Fabric Selections

After examining your collection of difficult fabrics, do you find a recurring selection pattern? Do you choose fabrics which consistently fit into one or two particular groups? If so, be aware of this selection problem on your fabric buying trips.

Look at your past quilts or textile art. Have some projects had disappointing results? If so, try to analyze the problem. Have you used any problem fabrics? If so, did they have a negative effect on the total visual image? Have you varied the scale of the fabrics used? Analyze your past choices and think how you might have selected differently.

When you shop for fabric, make a deliberate attempt to eliminate buying patterns which result in choices that are detrimental to your artwork. It takes time to change buying habits that have developed over several years. When fabric shopping, it's easiest if you decide before you enter the store what type of fabrics you will look for.

Figure 7-5 Highly Contrasting Prints
Highly contrasting prints tend to pull out visually,
taking away from the unity of a design.

Then, if you change your mind about fabric selection in the store, you can think consciously about whether you have made a great spontaneous decision or whether the choice is based on habit.

FABRIC USE AND SPECIAL EFFECTS

There may be times when you want to create a special effect in your art that can be promoted by using certain types of fabrics or fabric designs. Then again, there may be effects you want to avoid; you can reduce their appearance with specific types of fabrics. Here are suggestions for these purposes.

Depth

The scale of the prints you use plays an important part in illusions of depth. The largest print scales should be placed in the foreground or in the closest design elements. As your design moves into the middle area, scale size should diminish. Background fabrics can be quite small in scale, or may also be made from blurred or ambiguous designs.

Overall scale of patterned fabrics in the middle distances is usually smaller than in the foreground. However, you could use the backside of some foreground fabrics, if the color and value work and the design or texture is less pronounced.

Mottled fabrics, painterly fabrics, solids, or the backside of fabrics that give an unclear hint of a design are all good choices for background fabrics (photos 31, 34).

Iridescence and Opalescence

Fluorescent-colored fabrics work very well for iridescence. Also, fabrics that contain splotches of brilliant pure colors are excellent for this illusion, set against dark shades or black (photos 44, 65). For backgrounds, dark, rich velvets and velveteens provide an excellent contrast to brilliant iridescent hues. In special designs, silks or lustrous fashion fabrics like taffeta help evoke iridescence.

Muted decorator fabrics with soft, subtle overall designs are wonderful background fabrics for opalescent effects. Background fabrics used for opalescence should have designs that blur into one another, overlapping colorations much the way the mother of pearl does. Spring fabrics in clear tints are excellent choices for the sparkle of fleeting hues in opalescence (photos 44, 51).

Movement

Any fabrics that bring about a good flow of color are wonderful to depict movement. Fabric designs in which colors fade in and out, giving a painterly effect, are excellent choices. Mottled fabrics with soft color changes work well for color motion. Fabrics which promote unclear, blurred impressions can also be used

quite successfully (photos 34, 53). Sharp edges in fabric designs hamper the illusion of movement. Likewise, static prints are not usually appropriate.

Optical Mixing

When you use small amounts of solid fabrics together, you can often achieve optical blending, or the visual creation of colors that actually don't exist in the fabrics. This enhances your design's beauty. Seminole piecing and strip piecing are two of the most effective ways to make your own fabric for optical mixing. The fabric pieces must be small enough to allow the colors to interact with each other. Landscape quilts are enhanced by optical blending when the strip widths are consistently narrow. For best results, make your own fabric by combining colors in the same manner a painter would to achieve optical mixing (page 24; photos 19, 30, 75).

If you use fabrics of the same fabric content, like 100 percent cotton, it is easier to achieve this illusion than when you combine two dissimilar fabric blends. This is because unlike fabrics reflect and absorb light differently.

Reflections

You can use fabrics to show wind or water movement. A reflection made from identical fabrics used for the reflected object, in mirrored-image fashion, usually elicits a feeling of glassy water. If you want the reflection to seem somewhat lighter, try using the backside of those fabrics for a more muted effect. At times you may use fabrics that are not part of the reflected object. For instance, fabrics that only hint of the design or seem visually abstract or blurred suggest wind or choppy seas, or elicit an impressionistic feeling.

Simultaneous Contrast

You achieve simultaneous contrast more easily with solid colored fabrics. Print fabrics reduce your ability to attain this effect because it is more difficult to see an afterimage when the area is surrounded by small printed patterns.

Transparency

Transparencies are best achieved with solid colored or painterly fabrics (photo 86). Calicos or other pronounced prints make it difficult to trick the mind's eye into believing transparency is present (photo 47).

FABRICS REQUIRING SPECIAL TREATMENT

Most quilters and textile artists use cotton fabrics. Also, most fabric designs are fairly easy to use successfully. However, there may be times when you would like to expand your options and use lovely fashion fabrics such as velvets and silks, or difficult prints such as plaids and stripes. This section provides important information about fabrics that require special treatment in design, layout, or construction because of their makeup or design.

Napped, Piled, and Textured Fabrics

Certain fabrics, such as napped or piled fabrics, textured fabrics, plaids, border prints, and stripes, require special treatment. Directional designs work best in a design when their direction is consistent throughout the entire surface of a design. Ignoring these fabrics' directional qualities during cutting invites visual disaster for the final project. Suggestions for basic layout guidelines are included below.

Piled fabrics include corduroy, velvet, and velveteen. These fabrics have a definite direction or nap and are considered one-way fabrics. Determine the fabric's direction by running your hand across it to find which way it feels smoother. When your hand runs softly over the fabric, it is following the direction of the nap.

As a guide, remember that when the nap is up, the piled fabric appears rich, dark, and at its most intense level. If the nap is down, you will see a lighter, shinier cloth. As you move your position, the cloth's appearance changes if there is a change in the nap's direction.

Your first step is to determine whether to cut for the rich, dark effect or for the lighter, shinier look. Place your templates on the fabric in the identical direction they will be placed in your design. To obtain the exact grain line with each pattern piece, check your layout with a T-square before cutting. Remember that you cannot place your templates on the fabric for cutting in the same direction unless each pattern piece in the design lies in that same direction (figure 7-6).

To sew piled fabrics (napped), use a fine needle set at 10 to 12 stitches per inch. Always sew in the direction of the nap. Pinning is essential; hand basting at the seamline may be needed, because slippage is a problem. When sewing two different fabrics together, piled fabric slips less when placed on the bottom of the pair. You must sew a zigzag or overcast stitch at every seam edge to prevent fraying. Press on a deeply piled towel or a needle board (never press from the front side). To take out wrinkles, steam the fabric near a hot running shower for several minutes.

Satin, brocades, and other similarly textured fabrics must also be treated with care because they are directional. Light reflects off the surface differently, allowing for a shaded effect. For the most pleasing use of these fabrics, cut pattern pieces so that their direction in the design is always with the nap.

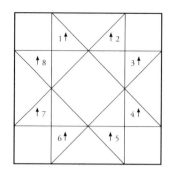

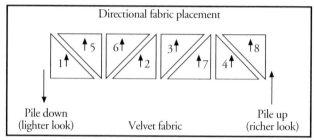

Directional fabric placement

Pile down (lighter look)   Velvet fabric   Pile up (richer look)

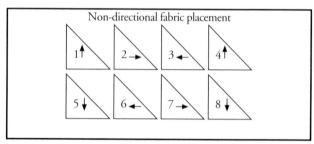

Non-directional fabric placement

Figure 7-6 Template Placement with Directional Fabrics
A. With directional fabrics such as velvets, place templates for cutting the design elements in the same direction on the fabric yardage as the elements will be positioned on the overall design.
B. If set in the usual fabric placement, the directional fabric will be disunified and distracting in the total design.

Other fabrics that need special attention are those that have lustrous, smooth surfaces that give subtle color changes. Silks, moiré, and polished cottons fall into this group. Cut pattern pieces from these fabrics so that their direction is consistent in the surface design.

Even some solid cotton fabrics show slight color changes when layout of the pattern pieces is not directionally uniform; so place pattern pieces on the fabric with the same care and guidelines required in dressmaking. That way you won't find any unexpected surprises when your quilt is finished.

PLAIDS, STRIPES, AND CHECKS

Plaids, stripes, and checks need special consideration when they are incorporated into a surface design. If their use is well planned, they enhance the visual outcome (photos 35, 36, 55, 58, 63, 75). But without planning, their effect on art can be disastrous. The following information is a basic guideline for using plaids, stripes, and checks. Once you understand the basic rules for using these fabrics, you may choose to be more carefree and innovative about your fabric design placement. When creating with these fabrics, do it carefully.

Because plaids, checks, and stripes present an additional element with their strongly placed directional or geometric designs, only use them to enhance the design. As a general rule, avoid using them with designs that involve complicated piecing. Make certain the scale of the plaid, check, or stripe is in keeping with the size of your pattern piece. An overly large directional design can draw too much attention.

Plaids

A plaid design is made up of stripes that cross each other at right angles. Some plaids are woven, while others are printed on the fabric. Do not buy a printed stripe, check, or plaid that is strongly off grain—or one that is not straight. If you do, you will fight the design during construction.

Plaids are designed as either even or uneven. In an even plaid the stripes are identical, both horizontally and vertically. When they are repeated they form a square with everything matching in all directions. In an uneven plaid, design and spacing are different in one or both directions; the colors and background do not match in both directions. An uneven plaid is much more difficult to work with than an even plaid, because it is much easier to make errors matching the design with other pieces. To choose the design placement of an uneven plaid, first determine which stripes in the design you wish to emphasize, and then remain consistent throughout the construction process.

When using plaids in a symmetrical design, place each template in an identical position on the fabric, so that all plaids will match within the design. If you are going to use plaids in different ways throughout your design, be careful with the layout, because plaids going in a variety of directions can be visually distracting.

Stripes

Stripes are easier to work with than plaids because the design runs in only one direction. In a symmetrical design, stripes look best if they follow the same directional pattern. If your fabric contains different widths of stripes, designate the dominant one and determine where it should be placed in your pattern piece. Sometimes several stripes closely set together, rather than just one stripe, take on the dominant role.

Stripes are balanced or unbalanced in design. A balanced stripe design is easiest to work with since it can be centered so that the repeat becomes a mirrored image. An unbalanced stripe will not give this same balance, if the area of the design is identical. It is best, then, to choose balanced stripes if you want to center the stripe and provide a mirrored-image effect.

Checks

There are very few good uses for checks in the realm of surface design. However, an appliqué woven basket may be a perfect design for a check fabric. If you have a specific idea in mind, and a check fabric works best, use it. Otherwise avoid using check fabric, as it can be distracting in your design.

THE QUILTING LINE: ANOTHER SURFACE DESIGN ELEMENT

Quilting lines can create an image, set a mood, or promote an idea. The quilting lines and surface design form an interlocking visual partnership that often intensifies an artwork's overall design. Although quilts can be quite stunning without quilting, this extra dimension gives you the opportunity to add further details, texture, and depth to your design.

American quilts almost always include a quilting design, which is either done by hand or by sewing machine. In many other countries, however, quilting is neither a tradition nor considered a necessary design component. Therefore it is often not included, or is used minimally. Batting, or wadding, is often not easily available to many patchworkers throughout the world. Furthermore, the batting can be extremely expensive, making it economically unwise to use. In the end, as in all design decisions, the choice of whether to quilt or not is an individual matter. The decision generally reflects personal preference, traditions, and the availability of batting.

The Quilting Design: Looking for the Less Obvious Line

As you work on your surface design, allow your mind to wander, vaguely thinking about ways to use the quilting line in your design. As you relax, ideas should begin to flow from your subconscious mind. Keep notes on any ideas you particularly like, as it is easy to forget them. When choosing which design to use, select the quilt design that either best accentuates the color use or enhances the surface design.

When you have completed construction of the surface design or quilt top, place it on a wall for several days, if possible. The longer you observe the design as it hangs on the wall, the more quilting ideas will come forth. At times, the first idea to come to mind seems best. At other times, you will have several excellent ideas and then have to decide which one to use. In other words, there is usually no "right" way to quilt your surface design.

When you enhance a surface design through the quilting line, try to create a secondary design line rather than simply reiterate the already-defined surface design. Look at the quilting design from all different angles to find a point of view in the surface design that differs from the obvious. After you take the plunge to quilt beyond the obvious pattern lines, you will find that your designs come alive with more exciting design elements. Your first successful attempt at using innovative quilting designs will probably spur you on to continue finding creative secondary designs in your surface design.

Study some of the quilts in this book which take quilting lines past the reiteration of pattern pieces (photos 30, 79, 82). Give yourself permission to let your creative mind explore new ways to quilt. You'll have a great time if you do. Enjoy exploring the quilting line, bringing new dimensions to your overall design.

With regard to the quilting design, regardless of our individual beliefs, it is important for each of us to accept the traditions and personal decisions of others. We should not feel that everyone must follow the same path. Instead, quilt or textile art should be appreciated for its beauty and its overall statement, not for the process used—or not used.

You, as the artist, choose how much, if any, quilting to do on your surface design. Some designs call for intricate quilting patterns, while others look best with a moderate amount. For certain designs, quilting simply detracts from their visual statements. Beautiful textile art without quilting lines includes photos 21, 22, 25, 26, 37, 38, 56, 77.

"Paintings aren't made with doctrines . . . I have always been repelled by theories. My only merit lies in having painted directly in front of nature, seeking to render my impressions before the most fleeting effects . . ."

—Claude Monet
French painter, 1840–1926
The Impressionists,
Portraits and Confidences

"The main line to follow is just to put down what you see. Never mind your temperament or your ability in respect of nature . . . Those outlines done in black are quite mistaken. The answer lies in consulting Nature; that is where we find the means."

—Paul Cézanne
French painter, 1839–1906
The Impressionists

CHAPTER 8

Creating Beautiful Traditional Quilts

Most long-term quiltmakers acquire strong technical skills and can construct a quilt superbly. One area often overlooked while learning techniques, however, is design. The majority of us have had little instruction in visual design basics for traditional quilts. Unfortunately, this puts us at a definite disadvantage when we plan appliqué and pieced designs. This chapter, therefore, presents guidelines and ideas specifically related to basic visual design for traditional quilts.

DEFINING A TRADITIONAL QUILT

To help clarify and reduce confusion, we should define what a traditional quilt is and is not. Simply, "traditional quilt" describes a very broad class of quilts that have historically-based design styles. American traditional quilts have their genesis in colonial and pioneer times. Other countries may have quilts with their own historic roots. Quilt designs based on any of these antecedents, no matter what country they originate from, are considered traditional. This historical style is universally recognized and accepted as such. This means that an originally designed quilt, made in contemporary times, is still considered traditional when its design style closely corresponds to any subdivision of the historically-based designs we consider traditional.

This form of classification is a time-honored tradition in all areas of art. For instance, when we use the term impressionistic, we define art that corresponds in design style with that of the French Impressionists. Impressionism can relate to art created during the period when Monet, Degas, and the other original Impressionists were painting, or it can relate to any art that corresponds closely to that particular design style, regardless of when the art was created—even today. The same is true in classical and contemporary music and ballet.

In the quilt world, traditional quilts are broken into several divisions by design style. Some divisions are even separated into smaller subdivisions. Block designs (both pieced and appliquéd) are the most prevalent traditional designs used in quiltmaking. Other divisions include central focal point designs (e.g., Lone Star, Medallion quilts), overall designs (Trip Around the World), and specialty designs (e.g., Cathedral Window, Yo-yo).

If you create a new pattern or design, and the end result parallels one of the many divisions within the traditional quilt spectrum, your quilt should be considered traditional. If, however, your quilt shows no relationship to any historic design style, then by today's vernacular it is a contemporary quilt.

DESIGN OPTIONS TO CONSIDER

Although color is the main visual ingredient in a work of art, you need a well-planned design to make the surface design successful. In the quilt/patchwork world, there are literally thousands of designs currently available to choose from. We also have the option of incorporating two or more patterns in the same surface design, which multiplies our choices even more. In addition, you can make your own variations on a traditional design. It is no exaggeration to state that in traditional quiltmaking, design possibilities are almost endless.

Before beginning construction, think carefully about the choices before you, and set some design parameters. What do you want to accomplish with this quilt? Is the quilt for the bed or a wall? Will the function of the quilt influence the design you use? If so, how? Does the quilt have to coordinate with other designs and colors in a specific room? What are your limitations, if any? Answering these questions begins to formulate your ideas.

When planning a quilt, determine what area of growth you want to emphasize, if any. If your primary goal is to develop or increase your technical skills, keep the design and color concepts within your current ability level. If you want to create a quilt that incorporates a complex design, work in a technical difficulty level you feel comfortable with. When you want to achieve a challenging color illusion in your design, keep your technique and design at a reasonable level of difficulty.

Realistically, don't expect to learn or master more than one major concept at a time. When we ignore this learning principle and expect ourselves to combine new and difficult technical, design, and color concepts in the same project, we set ourselves up to be overwhelmed and frustrated. Therefore, decide which will be your major focus: technique, design, or color. Then keep down the

Continued on page 77

The Magical Effects
of Color in Quilts and Textile Art

Quiltmaking began as a functional craft, providing warmth, security, and traditions along with enjoyment and beauty. Although it was not their intent, early quiltmakers laid the foundation for a dynamic, viable artform. If these original quiltmakers were alive today, they would very likely be in the forefront of our field, continuing to experiment with design, color, and technique, while bringing us even more creative traditions. Certainly, they would be pleased to see the artistic and technical progress that has evolved from their beginning stages.

We are fortunate that our traditions are strong. Yet individual creativity is blossoming as never before. As in other viable artforms, our field's strengths can be attributed to many elements. Of greatest importance, however, is the fact that a large portion of the international quilt world embraces both past traditions and contemporary thought. Growth and change are natural evolutionary steps that help keep our love for quilts and textile surface design exciting and strong.

Today, traditional and contemporary color, design, and technical applications are being influenced and stretched by an explosion of creative exploration. If we are to encourage this creative quest in our field, we must not only be willing to give ourselves permission to pursue our own interests and self expression, but we must do the same for others.

Therefore, let us embrace the diversity that gives us strength, and extend opportunities for self growth and natural evolution to all who seek it in our field. If we can do this with joy and goodwill, we will give tomorrow's quiltmakers a strong history of traditions and diverse options to choose from for their own points of departure.

May you enjoy the colorful array of quilts and textile art exhibited in Color Sections Two and Three. These particular works of art have not only been thoughtfully chosen to illustrate the concepts presented herein, but have also been selected to inspire and intrigue your creative spirit.

16. Sentinels, 1990, 94" x 46"
Charlotte Andersen, Salt Lake City, Utah
Exquisite example of pictorial appliqué with pieced border, using the
shade scale. Collection of Dr. Dean Bawden. Photo: Ken Wagner.

17. Eternal Triangle, 51" x 51" x 51"
Rita Scannel, Killeagh, Ireland
Luster appears in high gloss in this beautiful
contemporary Log Cabin art quilt, using a
complementary color scheme. Photo: Ken Wagner.

18. Ancient Directions, 1990, 80" x 72"
Alison Goss, Hockessin, Delaware
Design inspired by Southwest Indian Acoma Pottery;
also has traditional quilt pattern roots, being a
contemporary variation of Double Pinwheel or
Turnstile. Permanent collection of the Museum
of the American Quilter's Society.
Photo: courtesy of Alison Goss.

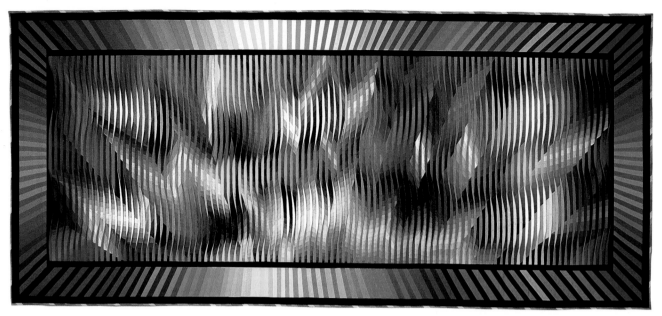

19. Aurora II, 1991, 109" x 48"

Caryl Fallert, Oswego, Illinois

Background in pure primary and secondary colors, which gradually fade into black and navy. The left sides of the tucks are many values of navy and black, fading to white. The right sides of tucks are a 44-color spectrum of highly saturated hues. The use of graduated colors and values, and the twisting of the tucks from side to side, create the illusion of light and movement across the surface of the quilt. Owner: Wilmette Public Library, Wilmette, Illinois. Photo: Jerry DeFelice.

20. Simply Kiwi, 1990, 33" x 26"

Diane Basch, Redmond, Washington

An organic original curved design, with innovative use of commercial fabrics. Photo: Ken Wagner.

21. Light Year, 1985, 156" x 46"

Suzanne Kjelland, Gig Harbor, Washington

A wonderful lustrous effect. Design made of triangles and squares. Owner: Jude Francisco. Photo: Ken Wagner.

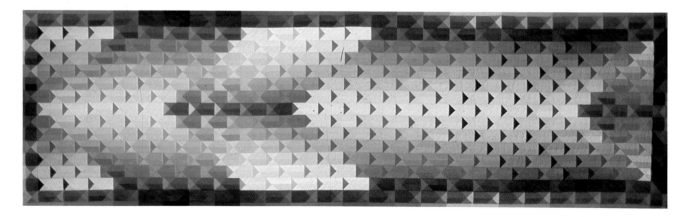

22. Yellow Iris Lawson's Pond, 1990, 59" x 47"

Amanda Richardson, Friday Harbor, Washington

A stunning example of textile art, using appliqué techniques without quilting. Reflection and luster are apparent. Photo: Patrick Kirby.

23. High Tech #32, 1991, 67" x 46"

Caryl Fallert, Oswego, Illinois

Background fabrics were dyed in primary and secondary colors. Each was dyed in graduated hues from white to black. Interlocking zigzags of black, white, gray, and rainbow stripes break the surface of the primary and secondary colors. An excellent example of color movement across the surface design. Photo: Caryl Fallert.

24. Autumn, 1987, 100" x 100"

Judith Tinkl, Sunderland, Ontario, Canada

A wonderful example of creating an overall contemporary design with a traditional block as the root (Pinwheel, Broken Dishes variations). With the shift of colors and values, the triangular elements of each block take on a minor role in this intriguing blend of colors. Photo: Saltmarche.

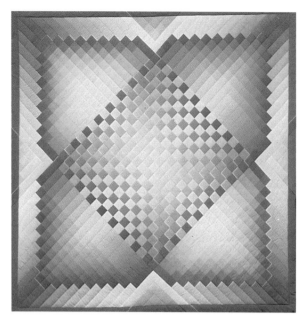

25. Summer Hill, 1985, 60" x 60"
Suzanne Kjelland, Gig Harbor, Washington
A symmetrical design created in the tint scale of complementary color families (turquoise and orange). Luster appears to exist with the subtle gradation of colors. Photo: Ken Wagner.

27. Georgetown Graduation, 1990, 23" x 25"
Joan Dyer, Redondo Beach, California
Excellent use of linear perspective using a traditional design. Depth is accentuated through blurred, toned background fabric. Squares and Stars block pattern variation, Georgetown, is designed by Judy Martin. Owner: Cheryl Dyer. Photo: Ken Wagner.

26. The Road Less Traveled, 1981, 49" x 77"
Suzanne Kjelland, Gig Harbor, Washington.
The toned, high-value color gradation covering the design surface promotes the illusion of mist. An excellent example of using warm hues from the shade scale. Corporate owner. Photo: Ken Wagner.

28. Bay Flight, 1988, 55" x 67"
Eileen Sullivan, Columbia, North Carolina
Innovatively designed and pieced quilt using blue and its complement, orange, in both toned (beige) and shaded (brown) variations. Tone scale is dominant. Photo: Ken Wagner.

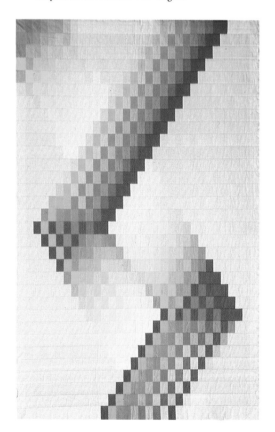

29. Butterflies Emerging, 1990, 65" x 53"
Patty Bently, Portland, Oregon
Original design created from two block patterns.
Well-planned fabric selection and color placement create
wonderful illusion in garden. Private owner.
Photo: Ed Dull.

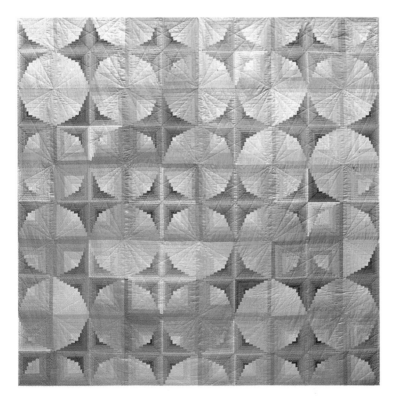

**30. Mellow Morning in the Forest, 1987,
112" x 112."**
Joen Wolfrom, Fox Island, Washington
An off-set Log Cabin design. Random color placement
helps achieve opalescent effect. Quilting lines enhance
design. This quilt was inspired by the work of Maria
McCormick-Snyder. Her exquisite off-set Log Cabin quilts
brought extreme interest to this Log Cabin variation in the
early 1980s. Private owner. Photo: Ken Wagner.

31. View from My Childhood Garden, 1988, 64" x 84"
Joen Wolfrom, Fox Island, Washington
Impressionistic strip-pieced landscape. Depth is achieved by placing toned, lighter-valued hues in the background. Owner: Ulster Folk & Transport Museum, Northern Ireland. Photo: Ken Wagner.

32. Oase, 1990, 140cm x 148cm
Rosemarie Guttler, Kuppenheim, Germany
Soft subtle tints are used beautifully to create impressionistic picture of a stand of trees. Photo: courtesy of Rosemarie Guttler.

33. Spring Fever, 1990, 46" x 46"
Mary Morgan, Little Rock, Arkansas
Beautiful color movement using triangles as the design element. Shade scale is used predominantly. Photo: Ken Wagner.

34. September Falls, 1988, 52" x 70"
Janice Richards, Gig Harbor, Washington
An impressionistic picture of salmon jumping a waterfall on the way to their wilderness spawning ground. Fabric choices and fractured blocks add interest and vibrancy. Photo: Ken Wagner.

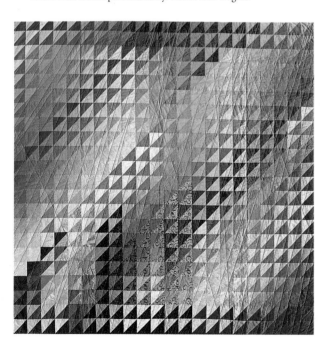

35

36

35. Landfall, 1985, 80" x 72"

Nancy Halpern, Natick, Massachusetts

Beautiful impressionistic design created in the toned scale. Quilting lines enhance the design.
Photo: David Caras.

36. Harborscape, 1989, 70" x 42"

Janice Richards, Gig Harbor, Washington

An abstract vision of Gig Harbor Bay, using fractured blocks to achieve the illusion.
A split-complementary color scheme evokes serenity while adding small color accents.
Photo: Ken Wagner.

37. Still Water, 1991, 62" x 100"

Karen Perrine, Tacoma, Washington

Beautiful blend of analogous colors creates serenity in this reflected scene. Color placement
in water gives impression of water movement. Photo: Mark Frey.

38. Riverside Iris, 1990, 13'6" x 4'

Amanda Richardson, Friday Harbor, Washington

Gorgeous scene showing reflection is created through
fabric and color manipulation. Split-complementary
colors evoke a peaceful mood in this nature scene.
Owner: Daniel Corporation, Virginia.
Photo: Patrick Kirby.

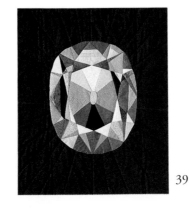

39. The Gem, 1992, 12" x 15"

Marion Marias, Fresno, California

A small quilt replicating an exquisite gem. The jewel-
tone hues interact with the lustrous sheen of tints,
appearing iridescent. Transparency also appears as the
colors seem to move. Photo: Ken Wagner.

39

37

38

40. Western Washington Tribute, 1988, 50" x 50"
Laura Reinstattler, Mill Creek, Washington
Wonderful example of a split-complementary color scheme. Effective highlighting using tints. Optical mixing occurs because intense hues are placed closely together in narrow strips. Private owner. Photo: Ken Wagner.

41. Raggedy's Rainbow, 1991, 86" x 86"
Nancy Billings, Miami, Florida
An original design created using the color wheel as a theme. The primary triadic color scheme is used, with many hues appearing to be transparent. Photo: Dan Loffler.

42. Migration, 1990, 48" x 36"
Caryl Fallert, Oswego, Illinois.
Both the bird shapes and the background were string pieced with fabrics dyed in both hue and value gradations. The birds were appliquéd over the background, with the backs of their wings partially three dimensional. Owner: Malinda Jones. Photo: Jerry DeFelice.

43. Luminosity I, 1991, 28" x 28"
Virginia Freal, Everett, Washington
A lovely color-wash design using a blend of colors and values placed together in small squares. Many such designs have been inspired by the work of Deidre Amsden of England. Owner: John Freal. Photo: Ken Wagner.

44. Tripping Around the World in a Splash of Color, 1992, 96" x 86"

Joen Wolfrom,
Fox Island, Washington

A favorite traditional pattern has a contemporary look with innovative color and fabric use. Luminosity is achieved by clear colors adjacent to toned hues. Iridescence appears as touches of pure hues are set among dark shades and black. Opalescence is achieved by touches of tints near soft, high-valued tones. Design elements are one-inch squares (postage stamp).
Owner: Danielle Wolfrom.
Photo: Ken Wagner.

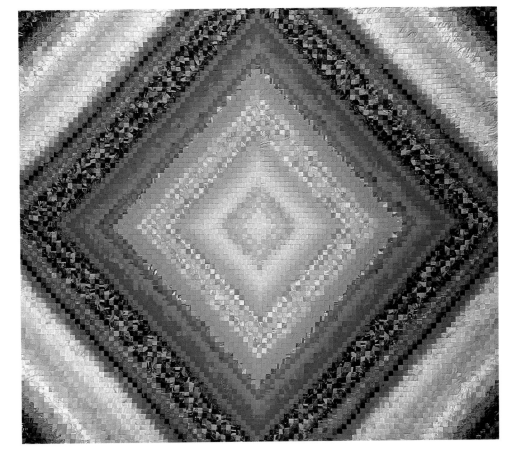

45. Oblique Illusion, 1992, 56" x 52"

Martie Huston, Santee, California

A superb creation of depth, highlights, and shadows. Large floating form with small boxes attached is such a strong illusion that it is easy to miss the traditional pattern in the box's background. (Similar background pattern as in photo 51.) Photo: Ken Wagner.

46. Galactic Color Wheel, 1992, 47" x 53"

Martie Huston, Santee, California

An illusionary color wheel of floating forms. Shadows and highlights are used. Cone sizes change, increasing the illusion of depth. Photo: Ken Wagner.

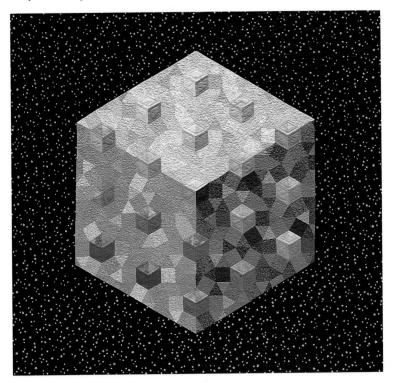

47. Log Cabin Series I,
 1989, 104" x 104"
Grania McElligott, Naas, Ireland
An unusual Log Cabin quilt set on-point.
Clear hues set against tones gives the fluting
effect in the center of the quilt. A color and
its afterimage make a beautiful statement.
Owner: Sean T. McElligott.
Photo: Tony Hurst.

48. Daleah's Sylvan Shimmer,
 1992, 25" x 42"
Pat Magaret, Pullman, Washington
Fanning flowers appear lustrous as gradations
of color are set against a toned background.
Inspired by Daleah Thiessen.
Photo: Ken Wagner.

49. Opals in the Web, 1991, 29" x 29"
Pat Magaret, Pullman, Washington
Design is based on traditional Spiderweb pattern. Opalescent coloring gives the
quilt a contemporary quality. Photo: Ken Wagner.

50. Crosscurrents, 1988, 61" x 42"
Alison Goss, Hockessin, Delaware
Beautiful, impressionistic scene created in horizontal and vertical strips. Depth is enhanced by toning and lightening hues as elements recede. Owner: Mary Lou Schwinn.
Photo: courtesy of Alison Goss.

51. Tears: A Healing Quilt, 1991, 55" x 72"
Judy Dales, Boontown Township, New Jersey
A beautiful, original design of subtle opalescence, using tints for the soft fleeting colors against a toned background. Background design's traditional pattern is understated with the superb fabric selection and value use. (Similar background design as in photo 45.)
Photo: Photographic House Inc.

52. Third Eye, 1985, 169cm x 169cm
Evelyn Montague, Cork, Ireland
A lovely original design using symmetry, with cool analogous colors enhanced by the warm center in a split-complementary color combination. Luminosity is created by surrounding clear yellow with toned hues. Private collection. Photo: courtesy of Evelyn Montague.

53. The Start, 1991, 30" x 24"
Judy Dales, Boontown Township, New Jersey
Inspired by a painting by William Scheeler. Color use is superb, effectively promoting the vision of wind, overlapping sails, and speed. Photo: Photographic House Inc.

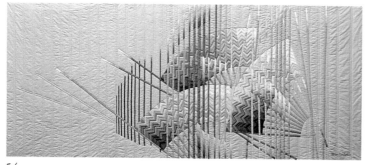

54

55

56

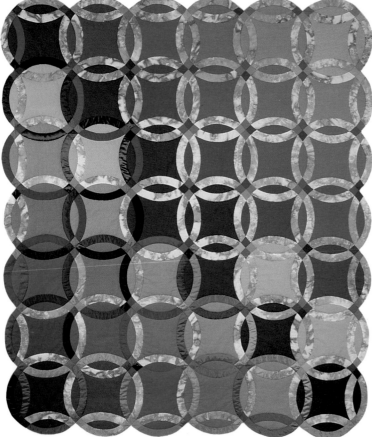

54. Three Fans, 1987, 114" x 48"
Laura Reinstattler, Mill Creek, Washington
Exquisite color manipulation in this beautiful toned design. Excellent example of complementary color scheme. Private owner. Photo: Ken Wagner.

55. Plaid Illusion, 1991, 52" x 44"
Shirley Perryman, Pullman, Washington
Plaids and value changes effectively create spatial illusions; an intriguing design using a traditional pattern. Photo: Ken Wagner.

56. Fractured Wedding Rings,
1991, 68" x 78"
Grania McElligott, Naas, Ireland
Double Wedding Ring design using beautiful blend of fabric and values creates an exquisite quilt. Photo: Tony Hurst.

57. The White Moose, 1991, 52" x 33"
Karla Harris, Hope, Idaho
A lovely strip-pieced/appliquéd wilderness landscape evokes serenity with its subtle blend of hues. Photo: Quicksilver.

58. River Condos, 1985, 41" x 40"
Carol Ann Wadley, Hillsboro, Oregon
Blurred, toned background accentuates the condo structures. Wonderful use of plaid fabric. Owner: Public Services Building, Hillsboro, Oregon. Photo: Bill Bachhuber.

57

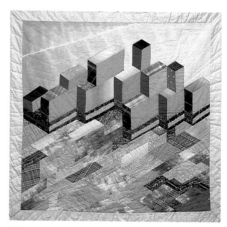

58

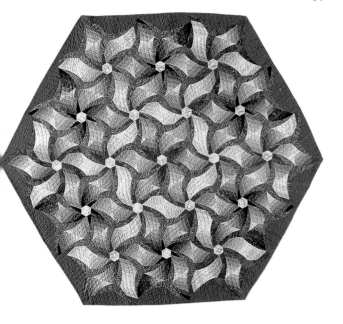

59. Satin Pinwheels, 1989, 82" x 82"
Joy Baaklini, San Antonio, Texas
Beautiful display of luster through color placement within a design.
Created in a monochromatic color scheme with values playing a
most important part in design. Photo: Ken Wagner.

60. Lattice Interweave, 1983, 84" x 84"
Miriam Nathan-Roberts, Berkeley, California
One of the most innovative original designs created in the early
1980s, this quilt exquisitely achieves the illusions of luster and depth
through wonderful color manipulation. Innovative border relates
well to the design. Photo: courtesy of Miriam Nathan-Roberts.

61. Starburst, 1990, 94" x 94"
Judy Sogn, Seattle, Washington
An innovatively-designed traditional quilt using a central focal point
design. The border enhances the design and promotes the illusion of
three-dimensional folds. Photo: Ken Wagner.

62. First Light, 1992, 52" x 67"
Nancy S. Breland, Pennington, New Jersey
A beautiful example of traditional design 54-40 or Fight variation,
using a monochromatic color scheme. The illusion of a starry sky is
well achieved with the change of values and the choice of fabrics.
Photo: Jay Turkel.

63

63. Kartenhaus, 1988, 148cm x 122cm
Friederike Kohlhaussen, Bad Homburg, Germany
A beautiful design with strong illusion of depth
through color use. A contemporary quilt showing
similarities to traditional Attic Window design.
Private owner. Photo: Courtesy of Friederike
Kohlhassen.

64. Glowing Pineapple, 1983, 46" x 34"
Diane Basch, Redmond, Washington
Traditional Pineapple Log Cabin design is an
excellent example of luminosity. The toned
fabrics around the clearer hues cause the latter
colors to glow. Photo: Ken Wagner.

65. Star Shower, 1990, 43" x 60"
Judy Dales, Boontown Township, New Jersey
Fabric selection promotes iridescent effect in
background. Wonderful original design, using a
star theme as a design. Intriguing use of plaids.
Photo: Photographic House Inc.

66. Latticeworks I, 1992, 32" x 32"
Carol Rothrock, Nordland, Washington
A beautiful color study with a three-dimensional
effect using the yellow/violet complements
advantageously. Photo: Ken Wagner.

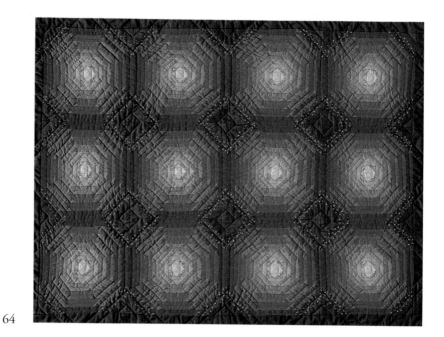

64

66

65

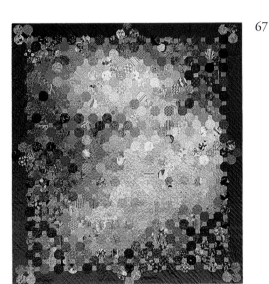

67

68

70

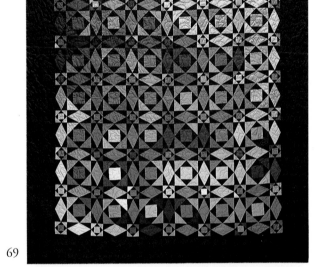

69

67. Arkansas Cobblestone, 1991, 83" x 89"

Martha Woodworth, Port Townsend, Washington

A traditional pattern creates a beautiful overall design when value changes are used for the main visual theme. Photo: Ken Wagner.

68. Out of Africa—Parrot Series #1, 1991, 37" x 25"

Geraldine Gahan, Dunlavin, Ireland

Strong geometric design created through color and value changes. Fabric choices add interest to design. Split-complementary color scheme creates excitement. Photo: Tony Hurst.

69. Storm at Sea, 1988, 86" x 96"

Sarah A. Dickson, San Antonio, Texas, and Maureen McGee, Lansing, Kansas

An exciting variation of traditional pattern Storm at Sea, with the color and fabric sequence changing in blocks, moving the design effectively through the entire design. Owner: Sarah A. Dickson. Photo: Ken Wagner.

70. Polished Plaid, 1991, 44" x 44"

Pat Magaret, Pullman, Washington

Gorgeous pieced and appliquéd quilt incorporating luster and depth through thoughtful color choices. Complementary color scheme is used. Influenced by Miriam Nathan-Roberts' interweave designs. Photo: Ken Wagner.

71. Trip Around the World, 1992, 48" x 48"

Lassie Wittman, Rochester, Washington

This traditional quilt zings due to color placement. Gentle hue gradations bring out lustrous effect. Photo: Ken Wagner.

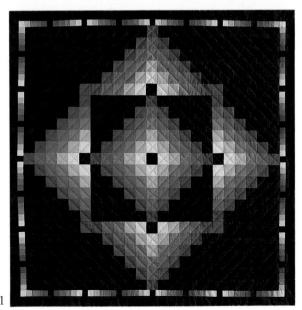

71

72. Globus, 1988, 62" x 66"

Erika Odemer, München, Germany

Wonderful illusions of depth and luster are created through color and design line manipulation. Many traditional blocks are set within the globe, superbly illustrating that block designs can be used in creating fascinating original designs. First place winner of QNM's international contest Visions of the World, 1988. Photo: Von Voithenberg.

degree of difficulty in the other two elements. Allow yourself to learn in small, easy steps; it is more fruitful than trying to learn everything in one project.

CHOOSING THE TRADITIONAL QUILT'S DESIGN STYLE

Take time to assess your design likes and dislikes. Begin by looking through books and magazines and going to quilt exhibits, and assess your reactions. Notice the types of quilt designs you are most drawn to. Do not confuse color likes with design likes. Once you ascertain your favorite styles, try to create only those quilts which appeal to your personal design sense. Several design options are listed for you to consider.

One-Block Pattern Repeat Design

Most traditional quilts repeat the same block throughout the entire quilt. Traditionally, colors and fabrics also repeat in each block. Quilts based on this practice are usually symmetrical. Their pattern, color, and fabric placement are some of the easiest to plan and construct.

If you choose to create a one-block pattern that repeats itself throughout the entire quilt, make certain you choose colors and fabrics that keep the viewer's interest. Although these are the easiest quilts to create, if fabric and color selection are not well thought out, the quilt's visual beauty is diminished.

USING COLORS TO MOVE THROUGH THE BLOCK

To add extra interest to a quilt with a repeat design, change the fabrics so they are not repeated in each block. Consider moving the colors and fabrics across the design surface so that they work into an interesting, flowing design. The color movement, rather than the individual block design, becomes the focal point. See "Gradation" (photo 84), created from the traditional Rail Fence pattern. The color arrangement leaves us unaware of the pattern except on close analysis. In the quilt "Autumn" (photo 24), with its roots from a traditional Pinwheel pattern, the play of colors across the quilt's surface supersedes the pattern.

CHANGING VALUES

Changing color values can add interest to your design. These changes sometimes stay within the block, but more often than not, the value changes meander throughout the design, paying no attention to the individual block boundaries (photo 69). Value changes can be both dramatic and subtle.

Two-Block Pattern Design

Alternating patterns in a quilt can create a more interesting design than a one-block pattern quilt. Using

Continued from page 59

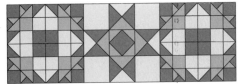

Figure 8-1 Combine Blocks with a Common Design Bond
A. When combining 2 or more different blocks for an overall design, use blocks that have a common design line bond. Weathervane and Braced Star are both 9-patch designs (block design grid divisions are divisible by 3). Therefore, they are mutually compatible as design partners.

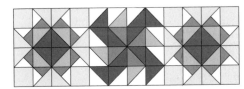

B. Missouri Star and Yankee Puzzle have a common design bond. They are both 4-patch designs (block design grid divisions are divisible by 4). They are mutually compatible as design partners.

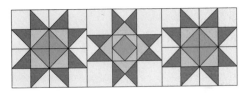

C. Blocks without a common design bond do not usually work well together in an overall design. Braced Star is a 9-patch design; Evening Star is a 4-patch design. They are not mutually compatible as design partners unless major revisions in design lines are made.

Weathervane Variation　　　Love in a Mist

Figure 8-2 Enhancing the Design when Combining Blocks
When you select two or more blocks to use in an overall design, enhance their compatibility by adding, deleting, and changing design lines so that the design flows from one block to another to create more interesting designs.

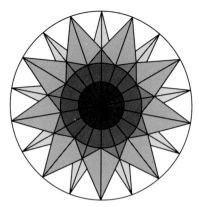

Figure 8-3 Traditional Quilt Designs and Visual Balance
A. Many designs radiate from the center, giving symmetrical balance.
B. Most traditional blocks are mirrored-image designs,
which give symmetrical balance.

Traditional quilts-
symmetry
Mirror-image pattern
Pattern: Star and Chain

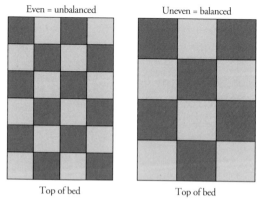

Even = unbalanced   Uneven = balanced

Top of bed   Top of bed

Figure 8-4 The Horizontal "Uneven" Rule and Bed Quilts
For visual balance, most traditional quilts should be planned so that
an uneven number of blocks lie across the width of the bed top. This
gives visual balance (log cabin designs are an exception).

two patterns can be most effective if thought is given to how the two patterns blend together, and to color and fabric selection. Choose blocks that fit together in a visually interesting and beautiful quilt. Blocks should not be easily distinguished by their individual parts. Therefore, some design lines of one block should blend into the adjoining block's lines, thereby merging the two. Large blank spaces in corners should be eliminated by adding design lines. The resulting design will be fascinating to look at and will appear to be more intricate than a one-block design.

Try to use blocks that have a common design bond. For instance, nine-patch designs work best with other designs based on nine-patch divisions. Four-patch designs work best with other four-patch designs. In both categories, designs can be further separated into smaller components (figure 8-1).

When you set two block patterns together, add lines, delete lines, or change the directions of lines to create a visually interesting design (figure 8-2). Sometimes this means playing around with the lines, using the eraser and white-out extensively.

Once you decide on a tentative design using two different blocks, make paper copies of each so that you have about 15 to 25 small blocks to play with (2" x 2" size is adequate). Then move these cut-outs around, setting the blocks in a variety of formations. Most often, designs are alternated in a setting. However, you may find some other setting that really piques your interest. Do not feel compelled to keep your blocks in straight lines, resulting in expected placements. Let your mind play and think up all kinds of ideas.

For an example of a two-block design set on-point, see "Butterflies Emerging" (photo 29). Not only is the overall pattern enhanced by using two subtly different designs, but the color and fabric changes within the blocks are fascinating.

Two-block combinations can elicit completely different quilts by changing hues, values, intensities, and fabrics. Take time to experiment so that you achieve the best possible combination to make your design into a dynamic quilt.

VISUAL BALANCE AND TRADITIONAL BLOCK DESIGNS

When planning a quilt, it is important to take advantage of good design principles. It is relatively easy to attain visual balance with traditional designs because they are almost always symmetrical. Most designs either radiate from the center or are mirrored-image patterns (figure 8-3). A traditional design can only be pulled off balance by inappropriate color choices, fabric use, or block placement within the total setting. Block setting is the easiest of these three elements to adjust.

The Horizontal "Uneven" Rule and Bed Quilts

With few exceptions, an uneven number of horizontal blocks gives the most balanced design for a traditional quilt (figure 8-4). Even when you set your blocks on-point, it is still almost always appropriate to work with an uneven number of horizontal blocks in a total design. Most traditional designs, then, should incorporate three, five, or seven blocks across the top width of a bed. (The most notable exception to this rule is the family of Log Cabin quilts, which needs an even amount of blocks for successful visual design.)

To help determine how many uneven blocks will fit across your bed, see the mattress chart on page 79. Decide how many blocks will best fit across the top of your bed (three, five, seven, etc.). Then divide the mattress width by the number of blocks to determine the block size. Once you decide the block measurement, you can draft the pattern to exact specifications. (See Appendix II for pattern drafting directions.)

Type of Mattress	Width Length
crib, six-year	27" x 52"
twin, regular	39" x 75"
twin, long	39" x 80"
double, regular	54" x 75"
double, long	54" x 80"
queen	60" x 80"
king, regular	76" x 80"
king, California	72" x 84"
king, dual	78" x 80"
king, water bed	72" x 84"

After you determine the size and number of blocks for the bed top, plan the design for the portion of the quilt which will drape over the bed sides. Decide how many blocks will extend over the side of the bed and how wide the border will be.

The Horizontal "Uneven" Rule and Wall Quilts

Many beginning projects are wall quilts made up of four blocks—two rows of two blocks across. When blocks are put in this setting, the design is almost always lost because our eyes automatically look to the center of a wall quilt. Thus, we end up focusing on the space between the block design, rather than on the design itself (figure 8-5). Consequently, the planned design takes on a secondary role. In essence, the negative space (background) becomes the active design while the positive space (foreground) recedes into an unnoticed area of shapes. For most traditional settings, the design is better served by a wall quilt three blocks wide, five blocks wide, or some other uneven number of horizontally-placed blocks. This way, you can see the center block's design (figure 8-6).

Two-Block Design Exception

You can set four identical blocks together and create a successful design by adding, deleting, and rearranging lines to create a central focal point design or medallion design. This is a completely different design process than placing four blocks together so that their less interesting corner design elements meet at the center of the quilt (figure 8-7).

Central Focal Point Designs

Many people like central focal point designs. Pieced quilt patterns in this category include the Lone Star, Medallion, Mariner's Compass, Giant Dahlia, Sunflower, and Blazing Star designs. Many appliqué quilts also

Figure 8-5 The Horizontal "Uneven" Rule and Wall Quilts
When four blocks are set together (above), the desired design is lost because our eyes automatically are drawn to the center area. Thus, the space between the block design (background), rather than the design itself, is focused on.

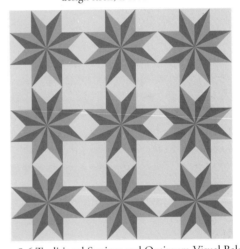

Figure 8-6 Traditional Settings and Optimum Visual Balance
For a wall quilt, set your traditional blocks in an uneven number horizontally to bring your focal point design into optimum view. You may also set your blocks in an uneven number vertically; this is not essential for visual balance with most designs. A design is usually best served when there are at least three vertical rows, however.

Figure 8-7 Four-Block Design Exception
You can set four identical blocks together and create a successful design by adding, deleting, and rearranging lines so that a central focal point design or medallion style design is created.

Figure 8-8 Beware of Border Overkill
Keep your borders in proportion to the design elements in
your quilt. The focus of a design should never be the border area.
If you have trouble focusing on the central area of the design
because your eye is attracted to the border, as in this design,
the border is too large for the design.

include a central motif that incorporates secondary designs to enhance the focal point. Some of the most beautiful designs are created from a central focal point (photos 52, 61, 79).

One of the most interesting and lovely characteristics of these quilts is their ability to incorporate more than one technique with ease. For instance, appliqué and piecework (patchwork) blend beautifully in a central focal point quilt. An appliquéd floral bouquet can be the center of attraction, with a pieced border of similar theme. The same theme could be reversed by placing a beautiful pieced floral theme in the center, rounded out by a flowing appliquéd spray of flowers, leaves, and vines.

OVERALL SURFACE DESIGNS

Many traditional designs that cover an entire quilt surface can become innovative, beautiful works of art. Study the traditional "overall-pattern" quilts that take on a new personality due to the way the artist has manipulated colors, values, and fabrics (photos 44, 67, 71). Next time you create a quilt using an overall pattern, consider the possibilities that await you when colors and values flow throughout the design.

ORIGINAL DESIGNS BASED ON TRADTIONAL PATTERNS

It is fun to create your own original traditional designs. If you have an idea, sketch it on graph paper or write a description on paper. Once it's on paper, give yourself time to think through a variety of ideas. Let the design simmer until it all seems visually comfortable to you.

While thinking through ideas, play with pattern lines. Adding, deleting, and changing lines adds shapes,

takes away shapes, and changes some contours of those shapes. Once you have a feeling for your design, make several copies of it so that you can work with the overall placement of blocks. Place the blocks side by side. Stand back from the design and see how it looks as a simple pencil drawing. You may want to rearrange some lines again, or you may want to add more shapes, or take away shapes—doing whatever seems visually pleasing. Again, let the design simmer in your mind. After some experimenting, you may decide on other changes. Your range of options is endless.

SAMPLER QUILTS

Sampler quilts are usually made from many different patterns. A quilt can easily be made up of 15 to 25 blocks. Although they are often used as a beginning project for first-time quilters, a sampler quilt is one of the most difficult designs to make visually successful. A sampler quilt is really best done by someone who has had experience manipulating design, color, value, and fabrics to achieve visual balance.

A visually successful sampler quilt needs unity throughout the entire surface design. Therefore, a unifying factor must appear throughout the blocks. A visually identifiable theme is one helpful way to begin. Choosing one, two, or three (or more) fabrics to weave in and out of the blocks is another way to promote this needed unity. If similar fabrics aren't used, consider repetitive coloration. Visual balance is also achieved by selecting designs that work well with each other. These designs must be placed in a setting that enhances the entire group.

One of the most important elements in designing a sampler quilt is the balance and the weight of each block chosen. It is extremely difficult to place appliqué and pieced blocks together in a visually balanced setting. Most pieced blocks are quite heavy compared to appliqué blocks, so blending the two techniques must be done carefully. Sometimes you can equalize the strength of the appliqué and pieced blocks by increasing the intensity or lowering the value of the colors used in the appliqué blocks.

Sampler quilts do not always have to be constructed with the same size blocks. To help achieve visual balance, you might make your blocks a variety of sizes, with an innovative one-of-a-kind setting.

TRADITIONAL QUILT BORDERS

A border's purpose is to enhance and complete the design. There should be continuity and unity between the border and the central theme. This continuity can be created through a theme or through line or shape repetition. Adding a new theme or shape may cause distraction

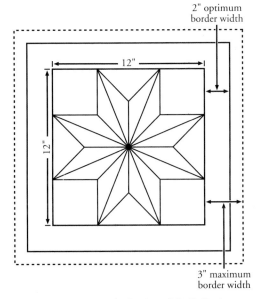

2" optimum
border width

12"

12"

3" maximum
border width

Figure 8-9 Border Ratio and Quilt Design
Try to limit your border so that the total width of both sides
is less than half of the central area. A border enhances
the design by framing it. It should be used as an accent,
not a dominant design element.

Beware of Border Overkill with Central Focal Designs

Even though central focal design quilts can be some of the most beautiful, the design proportions can plague the quiltmaker if she is not careful. When borders become too large, they overpower the central theme. If this happens, you have to force your eyes to find the center of the quilt (figure 8-8).

There is no written rule about the ratio of border to central motif for us to follow, and certainly each quilt has its own unique design elements to consider. However, you should keep your central theme the largest unit in your quilt. If the border is wider than half the central area, the border begins to overwhelm the focal point, or main design. Make the total of your two side borders combined less than the width of the central area (figure 8-9.) The colors, design, and size of shapes in the border can be a deciding factor in this ratio. If border elements are quite striking, you may have to decrease the size to compensate for a potential loss of visual balance. If the central focal point is brilliantly colored, perhaps it can withstand a larger border than usual.

Border Prints and Fabrics

As a rule of thumb, your border should include prints and hues from the main body of the quilt. However, sometimes you can use a solid fabric that reiterates the coloration of a print fabric already used. Without careful planning, adding prints to the border which are not included in the central part of the quilt can be disastrous; their incongruity will cause distraction.

That said, some quiltmakers have quite successfully broken all rules to create dynamic quilts with wild, wonderful borders. When they do so, they generally work intuitively and have had experience putting fabrics together in a successful manner. Through this experience, they understand the visual limits of their design and can work within their own guidelines. For most people, it is best to follow guidelines during developmental stages. Always be aware of the design, color, and fabric problems that can face you when adding borders, with or without breaking the rules.

rather than increase interest, so plan your border carefully. Additionally, the size of a central design should have a relationship to its border.

Although not all traditionally pieced quilts need borders, they generally enhance and frame a quilt design so that it looks finished. Some quilts, however, just need a simple binding. Log Cabin quilts, abstract designs, and landscape quilts are examples of designs that may look encumbered rather than enhanced by a border.

How you plan your border is a personal choice. Everyone's brain works differently. Some people plan their entire quilt, including borders, on paper. Others work from a fabric mock-up. Many quiltmakers work spontaneously, perhaps with tentative plans in mind which they discard at a moment's notice if a better idea comes along.

Border Size

If you add borders to your quilt, make certain that your ratio of block to border is appropriate. Keep each border less than one fourth the size of your block. For example, when working with 12-inch blocks, try to stay with a border that is less than 3 inches (figure 8-9).

Borders look best when the pattern pieces are the same relative size as those in the block design. If you have a 12-inch block divided into 4 parts, or 3-inch divisions, it is most visually pleasing to make no border pattern piece larger than 3 inches. Naturally, there are exceptions to all guidelines.

Innovative Borders

Some quiltmakers put mock borders on their quilts, incorporating a narrow strip several inches from the outside edge of the quilt, and then loosely carry the design out to the edge of the quilt. This is a very effective way of using a border to alert the viewer that the main body of the quilt has stopped, and the end is close at hand. It also keeps the continuity and size of the border well in control (See photos 19, 23, 34, 36, 42, 60, 84).

Some borders are so subtle that they seem like an extension of the quilt body. For example, "Butterflies Emerging" (photo 29) uses piping to make a small visible stop between the border and the quilt body. The colors and fabrics extend throughout the border, although the shapes change subtly. This border is very innovative and an excellent example of how to create unpredictable borders—yet it follows the guidelines of using colors and fabrics similar to those in the main focal area. It also maintains a size ratio with the rest of the quilt. "Globus" (photo 72) also has a subtle border that does not detract from the impact of the total design.

THE COLOR PLAN—
FROM MIND TO FABRIC

It is frustrating for many of us to put color to our paper designs, because we never quite end up with the same ideas on paper that we visualize in our minds. If making a colored drawing is a difficult, or impossible, step for you, perhaps your color visualizations are transposed more naturally through fabric than through paint or colored pencils.

Most of us work well with fabric in front of us, making our color choices while we manipulate the fabrics into the design elements. Perhaps our rough drawing will have scribbles of color for an idea, or maybe it will be labeled to give us clues to our color ideas. However, most of us will find that our thought process is complete from mental image to fabric because fabric is our medium. Certainly, we should not demand ourselves to first convert color ideas to another medium, such as paper, paint, or colored pencils before working in our own comfort zone.

CHOOSING COLORS
FOR YOUR DESIGN

Color is like magic, in a quilt or any other work of art. Even in fabric, color can be as fluid as in watercolor painting. Carefully chosen colors can elicit any mood. A dynamic design or a very quiet, subtle work can be created simply by manipulating colors.

In a dynamic quilt, your color choices will come primarily from the pure color scale. You could also have high contrasts in color with very little harmony between the hues used. Bright pure colors mixed together extemporaneously will always be more dynamic than colors that are consciously gradated into beautiful hues. A black background intensifies the other colors. Warm colors create art with more vitality than cool colors do.

By placing hues properly in your art, you can make colors dance or move around the design. They can also seem to vibrate from their placement. When you put an accent or a small amount of strong color, such as a pure color, among neutral or dark colors, it automatically draws your eye to that area. When you place a small amount of light color in a dark area, it creates a mysterious mood. This mystical effect can be accentuated by deep purples and blues. Graying colors tends to bring about a softer, more subtle mood.

Changing colors and values can be both spontaneous and predetermined decisions by the artist. Visually predictable color and value changes are usually preplanned, whereas quilts in which colors and values shift elusively often result from intuitive color placement done as the work was in progress.

"Autumn" (photo 24) has a planned feeling to its color placement, while "Opals in the Web" (photo 49) does not. Both use color and value changes to enhance their traditional designs (Pinwheel, Spiderweb). "Log Cabin Series 1" (photo 47) and "Mellow Morn in the Forest" (photo 30), both Log Cabin designs, illustrate the two methods of working. The former quilt uses its fabrics in a very organized, yet innovative, manner. The placement gives order and a feeling of symmetry. "Mellow Morn," an offset design with a contemporary flavor, evokes a feeling of spontaneity with its fleeting colors. No two blocks are exactly alike in this quilt.

When working spontaneously, you may find that your design begins to take on unexpected characteristics. An artwork can quickly change course simply through shifting colors. Your design may begin to appear three-dimensional. Perhaps you will find that some of your fabric positioning brings about movement or transparency you had not planned. When this happens, let your ideas flow and build your design from the inspirations brought about by fabric manipulation. The process comes alive creatively with unanticipated results that usually increase its beauty.

STRETCHING TRADITIONS—
GOING BEYOND THE ROOTS

Creative ideas come to us in an unpredictable fashion, without our being aware what stimulated the thought process or how our ideas grow once the initial spark takes hold. Some extraordinary contemporary quilts are inspired by or conceived from traditional design elements. These particular quilts could never be considered traditional, but traditional patterns must receive some credit, as there is a relationship between the two—although sometimes it is difficult to see at first glance.

Some spectacular examples of contemporary quilts with vague traditional roots include: "Ancient Directions" (photo 18) by Alison Goss, with its dimensional design based on a simple diagonal four-patch; "Harborscape" (photo 36) and "September Falls" (photo 34), two picture quilts by Janice Richards using simple block designs that are offset or fractured to achieve the design elements; "Oblique Illusions" (photo 45) by Martie Huston, where color placement creates a dynamic illusion of depth, and "Tears: A Healing Quilt" (photo 51) by Judy Dales, which uses the same basic hexagon pattern for its background with far different results; "Star Shower" (photo 65) by Judy Dales, an innovative design using the traditional motif of stars in a nontraditional setting—even the fabric use is innovative, with its plaids; "Kartenhausen" (photo 63) by Friederike Kohlhaussen, an innovative design related to the traditional Attic Windows pattern; "Globus" (photo 72), a magnificent work of art which utilizes star blocks from traditional designs changed through elongating the shapes and changing the colors.

As you can see from these examples, there are no boundaries or limits to letting a seed of an idea come into one's mind. Although these specific quilts may not have been consciously inspired or influenced by traditional designs, they do have a distant or vague relationship. Most assuredly, they are all magnificent examples of the creative process in action. Creative innovation, such as these quilts emphasize, is energizing, challenging, and rewarding.

Investigate design possibilities that pique your interest. Keep your ideas flowing and your attitude receptive. As you can see by many of the fine examples shown in this book, none of us knows what design potential is within ourselves until we allow it to come forth.

"I arrange my subject as I wish. Then I start to paint the way a child would. I want a red that will ring out like a bell. If it isn't like that, I add reds and other colours until I get it. I am no cleverer than that. I have neither rule or method. Anyone is welcome to examine what I use or to watch how I paint. He will see that I have no secrets . . . if a painting could be explained it would no longer be a painting; it would no longer be art."

"The work of art must seize you, envelope you, sweep you away. That is the way for an artist to express his passion; it is the current that springs from him and carries you away in passion."

—Pierre Auguste Renoir,
French painter, 1841–1919
The Impressionists,
Portraits and Confidences

CHAPTER 9
....

Creating Your Own Designs

Whether we realize it or not, each of us has our own unique design style. It mirrors our thoughts, our feelings, and our emotions, and reflects how we respond to our surroundings. No one else has quite the perspective we have about life, nor has anyone had quite the same experiences. Thus, intuitively, we blend our experiences and perspective with our innate preference for color, values, and intensities, and our natural bias toward or against harmony, discord, shapes, and lines. All these elements are carefully internalized in our creative brain, sorted out into a conscious idea, and then expressed in our chosen art form.

Your own artistry will be different from that of your friends. It may even be so strikingly unique that it is not acceptable to the mainstream point of view. That should not trouble you. Instead, your concern is to stay true to your own creative spirit. Wanting to create like someone else is self-defeating. You must simply create what reflects you. When you are in the initial stages of creative growth, it is important to take time to learn and to be around those who promote and encourage the evolution of your individual style.

You may lean toward fluid, flowing, emotive designs. Or, your style may be somewhat reminiscent of the elegant, yet unpretentious, Amish quilt designs. Your style may even translate into strong abstract designs with intensely colored and highly contrasting simple geometric forms. Your visual artistry may lean toward intricate piecing in a complex surface design. Or you may be challenged by the play of color and linear movement, disappearing, diffusing, and repeating its main theme across the surface design. None of these styles is necessarily "right" or "wrong."

Since your artistic expression is a mirror of yourself, your style will evolve naturally without you having to think too much about it. Simply by taking the time to create and to explore your artistic interests and possibilities, you will slowly find your design personality. Generally, everyone else will recognize your design style and color personality long before you even realize you have acquired them—you will be the last to know!

TAKING THE CREATIVE LEAP

During my childhood I was awed by the talent of several friends who excelled in art. It was then the prevailing view that an artist was born, not developed. So I assumed the gift of artistic ability was only given to a chosen few, and I was not one of them. Since I showed no outward display of being able to draw, I shunned every artistic opportunity provided in my formal education. I didn't see any reason why I should involve myself in anything that would be a certain failure.

Making a conscious effort to avoid art in formal education does not mean, however, that art is eliminated from life. Unbeknownst to me, art surrounded me and left a strong impact. It had been placed before me in a nonthreatening, informal manner—through nature, my home environment, and the cultural activities my family and community were involved with.

Now, of course, we know there is artistic ability in each of us, awaiting discovery. As you might expect, there is a catch to unlocking the door to individual creativity, however—the key only works when the right mental attitude is present. Creativity is very finicky, as it only develops under conditions of positiveness and self-belief. It refuses to come to light under negativity, extreme stress, and self-disparagement. It is also hampered when we are fatigued and unhappy. With that understood, we can say that creativity has the potential to blossom from a scant glimmer of hope into a full-scale, flowering career, if a person so chooses.

Our brain functions much like a miraculous computer. It does what we expect or ask it to do. Therefore, if we constantly tell ourselves we are not artistic, and we expect ourselves to fail at creative endeavors, our brain will prove us right. It is essential, then, if we are serious about becoming more artistic, that we never again consider ourselves without creative or artistic ability. Instead, we must encourage ourselves and believe that we are developing our artistic talents and improving our abilities. We must verbalize and visualize this creative journey, and truly believe in our abilities, even when they seem well hidden from us.

Every journey has a starting place, a destination, and a distance between the two points. In travel, we automatically understand that a trip includes planning, preparation, and movement from the place of departure to the final destination, with the possibility of some stops and side excursions as we travel. Therefore, the time spent getting to our destination depends entirely on the mode of travel and how long we choose to stay in any one place to investigate and enjoy along the way.

The same is true on your creative journey. There is a beginning point, a destination of your choice, and the total spectrum of unique possibilities between the two. Some people travel the distance in a short time, never veering from their original goal. Others make this a life-time journey. They spend enjoyable time investigating many avenues and find themselves exploring unexpected pathways. It's an individual determination how fast, how far, and how extensive your creative journey will be. The most important factor is, as in all journeys, that it should be fun, exciting, and fulfilling.

GETTING IN CONDITION

In its workings, the brain is also a little like other parts of our body—like our leg muscles. If we are not in the habit of using our legs, we feel strain after a long workout. If we decide to exercise our legs regularly, the strain ceases, and we are capable of much more than we expected. So it is with our brain. When we use it more, its ability and production increase enormously. Eventually, our creative imagination is filled with ideas we want to explore. Once turned on, it's hard to close the flow of ideas from our imaginative self.

Therefore, do not be discouraged if you have shown no artistic talent thus far. It simply means you have left a part of your brain untapped until now. That part will welcome the mental exercise of getting into good creative shape, and eventually it will show you what it can conceive and accomplish. Its possibilities are limitless.

BRINGING ABOUT THRIVING CREATIVITY

Creativity cannot thrive in a vacuum. It takes stimulation and good mental substance to produce good creative thought. Therefore, feed your mind with new ideas, inspiration, and numerous different types of experiences. Be willing to learn about what inspires you and sets your creative mind in motion by visiting galleries and museums. Scores of books from our immense interconnecting library systems can open the door to a vast wealth of knowledge. You need spend little, if any, money for these opportunities in learning, growing, and inspiration. We can experience the whole art world through a combination of activities at our fingertips, if we take the time to investigate what's before us. For the most benefit, give yourself the gift of a self-directed, stress-free, grade-free art education based on your own interests, time schedule, and needs. It will be a priceless experience.

CREATIVITY AND PERFECTION: AN UNLIKELY COMBINATION

A large part of creativity is dealing with new ideas and working with unknowns. It is a risk-taking process and consequently riddled with unexpected outcomes and unwanted mistakes. The best laid plans go awry; the most unexpected successes unfold before our eyes. It is almost impossible to enter the creative world without making both mistakes and discoveries. In fact, the mistakes usually lead to innovative techniques and vast strides in our artistic abilities. Therefore, we should look at mistakes as natural opportunities to further challenge our abilities.

Risking and making mistakes do not always sit well with us because they are generally against our upbringing, societal belief system, and the role modeling we set up for ourselves. We expect perfection from ourselves and from our peers. Hence, we put ourselves in a precarious, impossible position when we demand perfection of ourselves or others in creative endeavors.

In reality, perfection and creativity are diametrically opposed to each other. When we create something new, we cannot possibly foresee everything that will be presented to us. Therefore, we encounter problems that force us into taking risks and making impromptu decisions and compromises. Demanding perfection in such a situation is as unreasonable as it is impossible. We can only reach perfection when the course is well-known and predictable—when no new skill has been introduced nor any new idea investigated. Thus, when perfection is necessary, work with familiar techniques, designs, and ideas.

There should be a time for both perfection and creativity. Always setting ourselves up for difficult challenges leads to high stress and procrastination. Working only on safe, predictable projects that take no real thought leads to boredom and disinterest. We need a healthy variety from both avenues. After each major learning challenge, our next project should be an easy one where we can use our skills to perfection if we choose. While we work on the next comfortable project, our mind can be flowing with new ideas for the next challenge.

JUDGING OUR CREATIVE CHALLENGES

Creative growth keeps us energized. Our minds fill with ideas to put into surface design. We love the challenge of learning new techniques and presenting ourselves with innovative design or color challenges. Often, these innovative outcomes are quite compatible with the techniques and traditions of the past. However, sometimes these challenges may mean that traditional quiltmaking techniques or requirements are not attainable, applicable, or even desirable.

Some artistic accomplishments do not fit into traditional rules and expectations. Without creating a similar work, it is impossible for most of us to know if a particular innovative design can be made through traditional methods, or if traditional methods will have to be compromised, or even if new techniques are required. When a quilt doesn't meet the traditional standards or rules, it is important not to be too quick to judge the work negatively. We may find, instead, through investigation that the quiltmaker did an extraordinary job under the conditions she presented herself.

THE CREATIVE SEED AND THE INCUBATION PROCESS

Let design images play in your mind long before you begin cutting fabric when you attempt to create a new design. Conceptual imageries will take shape in a definite design idea through interplay between your subconscious and conscious minds, simmering advantageously for weeks, months, or perhaps even years. Allow yourself to think about refreshing alternatives. During this stage of design development, do not negate any ideas. No critical thinking nor judgments should be allowed during this creative thinking stage. You are ready to begin actual work when the ideas have played in your mind so long that you can visualize the design clearly in your mind.

Your visualizations will clearly determine your art's mood, thus dictating the dominant values to use. The choice of colors, patterns, and forms will also evolve. As you begin putting your ideas into concrete plans, your noncreative (left brain) judgments and opinions should be welcomed. Their construction practicalities need to blend with your innovative imageries to make your design both visually and technically successful.

Although an original design can be created without mental visualization, an intuitively inspired design will be a better reflection of your self-expressive mood and design style than art that hasn't evolved in this manner. Often, art designed quickly or in a forced manner (e.g., class project art) turns out to be merely an artistic exercise that lacks the spirit or soul of the artist, leaving both artist and viewer emotionally untouched.

Intuitive art generally elicits a response from the viewer. It may cause surprise and excitement, or it may suggest contemplation. It may simply evoke wonderment and awe. Or it may make the viewer laugh, cry, or become angry. Whatever the intended artistic statement, the viewer's response should correspond.

THE BASICS: ELEMENTS OF DESIGN

Even though art is highly personal, some generalities can help us think about the process of creating a design. Each art form has a beginning point of common language unique to its medium. The elements of visual design include line, shape, size (proportion), direction, texture, color, and value. These seven elements form the body of any visual design, no matter what medium is used.

Line

Lines can be either straight or curved in a design. Most designs in quiltmaking use either straight lines (photos 66, 79, 81) or curved lines (photos 20, 56, 59). However, designs can be quite successful when both types of lines are used (photos 23, 42, 53, 70). Sometimes straight lines appear to curve. The manner in which the design has been conceived brings about this optical illusion (photos 30, 69, 82, 86). In your design, there should be dominance toward either the curved or the straight line. Neither should fight the other for visual dominance.

Shape

A shape is anything that has width and height. Shapes are well used in the quilt world. Shapes include the active design, or positive space, and the background, which is considered negative space. They can be angular, curved, or geometric. A design is most successful when one type of shape has visual dominance over the rest. This dominance can be in size, shape, or number (photos 18, 22, 65, 66, 67, 70).

Size (Proportion)

In a design, shapes generally vary in size. There will be small, medium, and large shapes. Within a size, again, one should have visual dominance. When your design lacks variety in the size of its shapes, compensate for this by accentuating another element. For instance, if you have a design with all triangular shapes of the same size, the color and line movement should be powerful enough that the lack of size variation goes unnoticed. This can often be done quite successfully (photos 21, 24, 26, 33, 43, 44, 81, 84).

Direction

A dominant movement, or direction, should be apparent in your design. This directional force will move the design either horizontally, vertically, or obliquely (diagonally, or at an angle). Optimally the design should not remain static, showing no direction. A design's direction is most often determined by movement of either lines, shapes, or colors (photo 23, 26, 28, 33, 37, 84).

Overall shape of the art can also strongly influence the directional movement. For instance, art of a horizontal shape has a natural horizontal leaning (photo 38). To make the design move vertically, the upward linear or color movement must be extremely powerful to override the horizontal configuration.

A design that has an overall vertical configuration leans strongly toward a vertical direction (photo 37). Changing the direction to horizontal dominance demands a strong horizontal design line. The linear movement and color placement must work hard to negate the natural inclination of the art.

Art designed in a square configuration is the most difficult shape in which to achieve direction successfully because there is no natural tendency for the line to move either vertically, horizontally, or obliquely. If you have a choice, plan your art's configuration to be either horizontal or vertical, rather than square. See photo 43 for successful use of direction with a square configuration.

Texture

Texture is another design element we concern ourselves with in the quilt and textile field. We can create art that appears to be smooth, rough, soft, or even metallic through the illusionary process. Our choices of textural illusions can be created through color selection, fabric type, fabric placement, scale and print of fabric, fabric manipulation, and quilting lines. The latter can bring about forceful impressions of images. (See Chapter 7 for fabric details.) Remember not to put too many different textural changes in your design. Again, one impression should be dominant.

Color

Color is usually the strongest design element in an artwork. It is most often the major force in determining direction, shape, and overall design (photos 23, 26, 44). The most pleasing art has one color, or one color family, that is dominantly carried throughout the design (photos 73, 80, 85). When two colors compete for dominance, it becomes very distracting. Specifics of color in a design are addressed in other sections of this book (see Table of Contents).

Values

Values, or the lightness and darkness of a hue, bring about diversity of colors in a design. The highest values include the lightest colors; the lower values are used for the darkest parts of your design. Everything else is generally in the middle value section. In order to assure that your focal point does, in fact, stand out in the design, you must concern yourself with its value and the values of the hues around it. Likewise, the background values of a design are an important factor if you do not want the background to take over the active part of your design. Your picture should be planned so that a particular value key dominates (photos 25, 30, 32, 57, 76, 77, 79). (For more about values, see Chapter 3.)

PUTTING DESIGN ELEMENTS TO WORK

The seven design elements are used to form a unified artistic visual statement. As we are well aware, color, along with line, forms the theme and background of visual art. The other elements are brought into play to enhance and bring forth nuances that help create the complete visual story. In every design, these elements are stirred together in a unique fashion that brings forth its own individual quality. Thus, good design embraces, to some degree, balance, harmony, gradation, variation, alternation, contrast, dominance, and unity within these seven design elements.

The elemental design ingredients can be blended into four categories of visual relationships: repetitive, harmonious, contrasting, and discordant. Each relationship evokes a different visual statement, and each of us generally prefers one of these relationships over the others in our personal design style. Perhaps you will recognize the relationship most akin to your design personality.

A Design of Repetition

In a repetitious design, elements are identical. This is the primary design relationship of most traditional quilt designs. Repetition, if not handled carefully, can become monotonous. This easily happens if all elements—size, color, shape, value, line, and texture—are identical throughout the work.

The eye usually needs some relief from repetition; thus extra thought should be given to providing some change. Well-balanced repetition, which leads to harmony, can be attained simply by repeating a shape while changing the color slightly, or by changing the shape as you keep the same color (photos 49, 55, 56, 62, 81, 84).

There is a fine line between unity and monotony in repetition. Attaining unity without allowing the repetition to become too apparent is more an intuitive balancing act than an academic formula. With experience, you will attain your own sense of unity without too much repetition.

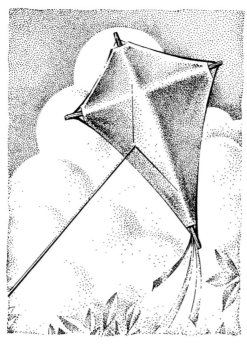

Figure 9-1 A Specific Focal Point

Figure 9-2 A General Focal Point

A Design of Harmony

If the elements within a design are not identical, but are similar, they are considered harmonious. Many traditional quilt designs also fall into this category (photo 29). If you would like to incorporate a degree of harmonious contrast in your design, consider incorporating gradation. Gradations are small steps that act like bridges between two extremes. Nature often uses gradations to bridge distinct differences, as in night and day, or summer and winter. Thus, gradation is a very natural way to work harmoniously with elements in our art. If you want to express subtle change and movement, gradation is a primary avenue to attain a harmonic illusion (photos 25, 26). Gradation can be used in any of the design elements.

A Design of Contrast

If the elements in a design are different in a pleasing or intriguing way, the relationship is one of contrast. Some contrast is necessary for art to be interesting and to sparkle. Contrast alleviates monotony without being extreme. You may simply change shape sizes or change the forms of the shape. You may also alternate shapes, colors, or lines. Color may provide contrast while the other elements remain similar. For examples of contrast, see photos 18, 54, 58, 61, 65, 67, 68, 70, 72.

A Design of Discord

In a design of discord, no elements are similar; the art is created in extreme contrast. Discord, then, is the opposite end of the spectrum from repetition. Discord can become a primary focus of an artwork if the artist wishes to emphasize disunity, friction, or contradictory images. This type of art is often created to make a statement and is not necessarily beautiful to look at. It is meant, instead, to be thought-provoking.

Traditional quilt designs rarely fall into this category. However, many contemporary works do use discord to convey visual messages. If you are trying to create beautiful art, watch that your design does not contain too much disharmony or discord. If you are making an artistic statement that invites discord, do not feel bound by any limitations.

MORE DESIGN CONSIDERATIONS

Other areas of concern that you will wish to address when you create your own designs are listed below. Each is important to the total design, so none should be overlooked.

A Focal Point

A remarkable work of art generally has a strong point of interest. This is considered the focal point. It is best to include only one major focal point in a design, since art is most successful when it visually expresses just one major point of view. If you include another focal point, make certain that it plays a subordinate visual role in the design. It should not compete with the major focal point.

There are two main types of focal points to consider. The first is very specific, being similar to the main character in a book. The design is developed around one major design element or feature (figure 9-1). This area can be emphasized by your color or value choices (photos 17, 22, 27, 28, 32, 52, 57, 72, 85, 86).

The other type of focal point is more generalized, but the focus is still very evident. This structure can be related to the main theme of a book, rather than the main character. This focus presents a broader spectrum of interest in the design. It generally encompasses most of the design surface (figure 9-2). No one specific element stands out in single glory. Instead, the presentation is more comprehensive (photos 16, 31, 37, 47, 56, 63, 68, 73, 78, 81).

Know which type of focal point you want to use in your design. Then determine what your focal point will be. While you draw your design, plan how you will focus on your featured design element or main theme. When constructing the design, make the focal point stand out in some way. This is generally done through color or value.

Determining where your focal point will be is a very important part of your design plan. With few exceptions, the focal point should not be at the midpoint of your picture, either horizontally or vertically. (Exceptions are certainly made when your design is based on a central focal point.) Instead, the focal point should be placed above or below the horizontal middle of the design, and to the left or right of the vertical center. Play with your design and see where your focus works best visually. As a guideline, locate your focal point where the distances between its center point and the four outside edges are all different.

Photographers often use the rule of thirds to set focal points. They divide their pictures into thirds, both horizontally and vertically. Then the focal point is placed near or on any one of the points of intersection (figure 9-3). This rule can also be used in your design structure to develop a feeling for compositions that are pleasing to the eye.

Do not allow this rule to supersede your own creative expression, however. If your visualization places the focal point of your design prominently at a point that does not follow the intersecting lines, follow your intuitive design sense. Guidelines are not meant to be followed rigidly. They are simply to be used when initial exploration commences. As you develop your style, your own sense of focal point and design setting will evolve.

A Dominance of Elements

For visual comfort, we need dominance displayed in our art. We feel discomfort when two colors fight for dominance. The same happens when shapes, values, direction, or any other elements cause internal strife between their parts. Each element needs one of its characteristics dominant. If this does not happen, the art becomes ambiguous or distracting.

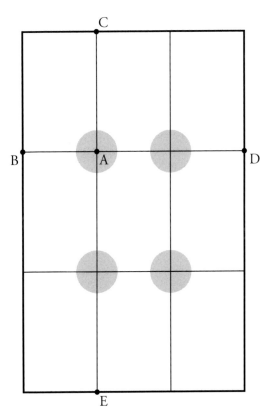

Figure 9-3 Positioning the Focal Point: the Rule of Thirds
Shaded areas show places of vertical and horizontal line intersections. These intersecting areas are suitable for placing a design's focal point. The distance between A and points B, C, D, and E all vary. This is a goal when positioning a focal point using the rule of thirds.

Visual Balance

Visual balance is a fragile design component. There is no set formula for achieving this balance in an abstract design. It can easily be destroyed by simply changing one shape's color, value, size, or placement. Visual balance is like a kite floating in the air. When the balance is perfect, it flies with ease, in beauty and harmony with the other elements. As soon as the balance is off, even slightly, everything begins to fall apart. The vision of all the elements working together in beautiful harmony is destroyed.

In traditional quilt designs based on a central focal point, the balance almost always works because these designs are symmetrical. However, if you change the design to create variation, the balance can change from a safe, formal setting to an informal, asymmetrical one.

When you are designing, stand back from your design to get a different perspective. Possibly use a reducing glass to see if your design's visual balance is accurate. Remember that creating exciting designs that involve asymmetry is always less safe than creating from a symmetrical traditional quilt design. However, the excitement of achieving balance in a challenging abstract design is worth the risk!

NATURE AS A MENTOR

Some designs achieve visual unity easily, while others seem to fight against it. Whether we are successful or not, each time we create a new design, we add to our repertoire of skills, techniques, and design experiences. Continue observing nature for design ideas and help. You will see that she uses all the visual elements of form: line, color, direction, shape, value, texture, and proportion. For instance, a seashell's lines form repetitious designs. These lines also form shapes that promote a sense of direction and proportion. Additionally, seashells elegantly display color and value changes. Texture, too, plays an important part in the beauty of the seashell. In so many ways, nature provides answers to our design questions. Fortunately, her beautiful designs surround us every day. Nature's designs can be readily used for inspiration and guidelines.

Artistic Unity

Unity is a sense of elements balancing in a cohesive design that expresses the ideas and emotions of you, the artist. It often takes time to develop art that projects a sense of individualistic artistic unity. As you develop the skills to position elements into visually successful designs, your personal style will evolve magically. Your art will then have its own individual mark, which cannot be taught or explained—nor can it be achieved immediately.

The way you put elements together into an artistic statement will almost always remain identifiable throughout your creative lifetime, even as your design style continues to evolve. Although you may wish for creative perfection, your personal creative package will never be complete as long as you continue to work in a creative manner. To embrace creativity is to welcome growth, challenge, and excitement in life.

PLANNING AN ORIGINAL DESIGN

Generally, when you begin working on a design, it will have been in your mind for a considerable time. It would then be relatively easy to begin playing with this design on paper. During this transposing process (going from mind to paper), do not be concerned with color or fabric. Although you may have general ideas about color and fabric, the specific hues and fabrics to be used will be decided as your design develops and progresses into the construction stage.

If you wish to begin a design, but have not had time to let the visualization process take hold, start playing with a shape that interests you (e.g., a tree, a starfish). This may be an actual object that is given an ambiguous form. Let yourself explore during this design process. Whenever possible, while creating an abstract design, avoid actual representation. Instead, attempt to project your own artistic interpretation onto the form. This design brainstorming process may take place quickly, or you may decide to play with the design for several days or weeks.

If you think you should not begin creating your design until every question has been answered, chances are you will never begin. Every part of your design does not have to be thoroughly thought out before proceeding with construction. Simply, if you have an idea, begin it.

The questions you have concerning your design, or unresolved issues of technique or fabric placement, should not be barriers to starting a design. Interestingly, all dilemmas that stand before you prior to cutting the first piece of fabric will most assuredly be solved as your work progresses. This evolution of creative problem solving is one of the profound talents of our creative mind.

Remember, too, that success is not a goal. It is simply a state of mind. Therefore, if your design does not quite evolve the way you had wanted it to, you have still been successful if you have learned at least one new idea or technique, if you have made at least one mistake that resulted in a new learning experience, or if you have made creative design progress.

Creating an original design is an act of stretching one's knowledge and abilities. It is a very concrete form of creative growth. Each project that you engage in will broaden your knowledge and experience, thereby increasing your individual design aptitude.

The thrill of creating an original design is not in achieving perfection, but in the challenge of transposing into actuality what our mind perceives. Equally as exciting is the prospect of discovering what our imaginative spirit holds for us as we evolve even further down the creative pathway. While we travel on our creative journeys, may our paths meet with joy. Best of luck in your creative endeavors.

> "What lies behind you
> and what lies
> before you
> are tiny matters
> compared to
> what lies within you"
> —Ralph Waldo Emerson
> American essayist and poet,
> 1803–1882

CHAPTER 10

Exercises & Activities

EXERCISE 1: CREATING YOUR OWN 24-STEP COLOR WHEEL

OBJECTIVES: While blending paints to attain the hues to complete a 24-step color wheel, you will see how colors mix together to form new hues. The finished color wheel can be a useful visual aid reference.

REFERENCES: Chapter 3

Supplies:

Liquitex Acrylic Paints® (water-based paints):
 Cadmium Yellow Light, Brilliant Blue, Magenta Medium

one or two 1" nylon brushes (medium priced)
tablet of watercolor paper, pencil
paint and water containers
blending and stirring utensils
black tagboard for mounting color wheel
compass, protractor, scissors (rotary cutter/board), glue
package of Letraset® Pantone Color Selectors (uncoated), paint chips, or appropriately colored papers

Directions:

1. **Divide the Color Wheel Painting Progression into Four Steps:**

A. yellow to turquoise   B. yellow to magenta

C. magenta to violet   D. turquoise to violet

2. **Yellow to Turquoise Hue Spectrum**

 Put a large amount of yellow paint into a container. Mix a small amount of water with the paint to obtain a good spreading consistency. Paint a swatch of yellow on a piece of watercolor paper (minimum 2 x 4 inch swatch). Then add a small drop of turquoise paint to the yellow paint. Make another swatch on the paper with this new color. Then add a few more drops of the turquoise paint to the yellowish mixture. Paint the next swatch. Continue to slowly add more turquoise paint to the yellow mixture, while making swatches after each addition. Work in this manner until the paint mixture is almost identical to the primary turquoise color.

 Selected hues from this group of color swatches will be placed in the yellow to turquoise span of the color

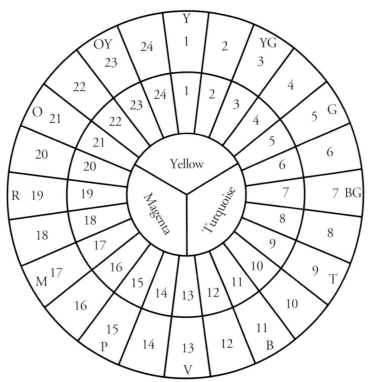

Figure 10-1 24-Step Color Wheel with Afterimages and Primary Colors

wheel. Between the primary colors of yellow and turquoise, there are 7 hue steps on a 24-step color wheel. It may be that you will actually paint 12 to 18 color swatches of yellow-turquoise mixture to obtain 7 good steps between these two primary colors. Try to make the gradations between the primary colors fairly even.

3. Yellow to Magenta Hue Spectrum

Beginning again with yellow, repeat the same color process as in #2. However, use magenta as your added hue instead of turquoise. (Use a clean paint container.) Continue slowly adding magenta to the yellow mixture while making new color swatches. Mix the yellow and magenta paints together until the color blend nears magenta. A selected group from these color swatches will be placed on the color wheel, ranging from yellow to magenta.

4. Magenta to Violet Hue Spectrum

Beginning with magenta, make a swatch of color. Then begin adding turquoise to the magenta paint. Continue adding turquoise paint, then painting swatches, until you attain a very dark violet hue. From this group of swatches you will pick three colors from magenta to violet to be placed on the color wheel. The color wheel violet may also come from this group.

5. Turquoise to Violet Hue Spectrum

Begin the same painting process, starting with turquoise. After making a turquoise swatch, add magenta to the paint, a little at a time. Continue to make swatches of paint after each paint addition. Again, when you reach a dark violet, stop blending the paints. Pick the three colors from turquoise to violet on the color wheel from this group of colors. The violet may also come from this group of mixtures.

6. Drawing the Color Wheel

With a compass, draw a circle for your color wheel base from the watercolor paper (or other background). You can make your color wheel as large as you wish. A helpful size is 8 to 12 inches in diameter. Divide the circle into 24 equal divisions by setting the protractor on the diameter line (matching center points) and marking every 15 degrees. Number the 24 divisions, starting with yellow as number 1. Turquoise will be number 9, and magenta will be number 17. All other colors will be located between these three primaries in a graduated order.

7. Placing the Hues on the Color Wheel

Determine which swatches you will use in your color wheel gradations. Place them in their correct color order, 1 to 24. Then cut the color steps from each chosen swatch using a plastic or tagboard template. Make the template slightly bigger than the drafted size. This slight overage will allow for overlapping colors so that no background white shows through. Glue the color steps down on the drawn color wheel. Mount the finished color wheel on black tagboard or other sturdy material.

8. Placing Afterimages in the Inner Color Wheel

For more color experience, place afterimages of each pure color in the middle 24 spaces of the color wheel. Use the Letraset® Pantone Uncoated Color Selectors or paint chips for finding the afterimages (see page 23 for directions on how to find afterimages; see photo 1). Place the three primary colors in the inner section of the circle.

Exercise 2: Blending Colors

OBJECTIVE: As a result of this painting exercise, you should have a better idea of what happens when colors are mingled and thoroughly combined. You should also better understand the relationship between colors after finishing this set of exercises. This is the initial exercise for building transparency skills.

REFERENCES: Chapters 3 and 4

Supplies:

Liquitex® Acrylic Paints (water-base paints):

Choose your favorite color paint (paint 1).
> Purchase this paint, along with its complementary color. Also purchase: Titanium White, Mars Black, Neutral Gray 5

two ½" to 1" nylon brushes (medium priced)

paint containers, water, utensils to stir

watercolor paper

Directions:

1. Blending a Color with its Complement—Toning the Color

Place a sizeable portion of your paint (color #1) in a container; mix with water to spreading consistency. As in the color wheel exercise, paint a color swatch of the pure color on the watercolor paper. Then drop a tiny amount of that color's complementary color into the mixture. Make two paint swatches: (1) with the paints mingled together in interesting blends, prior to mixing the hues thoroughly, and (2) with the paint and its addition thoroughly combined.

Continue adding more of the complementary color to the paint mixture, making two paint swatches each time you add more of the complement. Notice the beautiful richness of the intermingled colors. Also notice how the original color loses its vibrancy as more of its complement is added to it. Continue mixing and making swatches until you feel the color has become completely

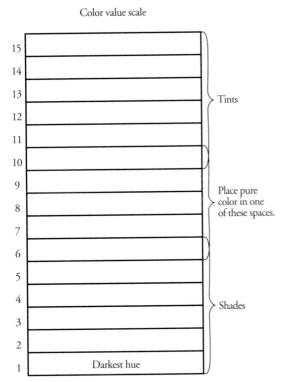

Color value scale

15	
14	
13	Tints
12	
11	
10	
9	Place pure color in one of these spaces.
8	
7	
6	
5	
4	Shades
3	
2	
1	Darkest hue

Figure 10-2 Color Value Scale
Based on your painted color swatches for your chosen color, select 15 hues that range from lightest to darkest in value. Position the pure color in the most appropriate space for your color range (between #6 and 10). Arrange the tints and shades in a graduated order. Cut and place on the scale so that the colors flow from the lightest tint to the pure color to the darkest shade. Repeat the exercise for the painted swatches of the complementary color.

neutralized. These swatches are the toned color scale of color #1.

2. Blending a Complement with its Partner—Toning a Complement

Now reverse the colors. Place a sizeable portion of the complementary color in a container. Add water for spreading consistency. Make a paint swatch on the paper. Then begin adding color #1 to the complementary color, a small amount at a time. Again, after each paint addition, make two swatches, one with intermingled colors and one with the colors thoroughly blended. Continue working until you feel the complementary color has become completely neutralized. These colors will be the tone scale of the complementary color.

3. Shading a Color and its Complement

Again, starting with color 1, place a portion of the paint in a clean container. Add water for spreading consistency. Paint a swatch. Then slowly add black to the paint mixture. Each time you make an addition, make two swatches of paint, one with intermingled paint and one with the paints thoroughly combined. Continue in this manner until you feel the paint mixture is at its darkest shade.

A color's tone scale

15	Most grayed
14	
13	
12	
11	
10	
9	
8	
7	
6	
5	
4	
3	
2	Slightly grayed
1	Pure color

Figure 10-3 A Color's Tone Scale
With your chosen color's toned painted swatches select 15 hues including the pure color. Keeping the color steps as even as possible, cut and position the hues on your tone scale, moving from the pure color to the most toned.

Repeat the painting of shade swatches with color #1's complement. These combined color swatches will be the shade scales for both color #1 and its complement.

4. Tinting a Color and its Complement

Start with a portion of white in a clean container. Make a swatch of white. Then slowly add color #1 to the white. After each addition of paint, make two swatches, one of intermingled colors and one of the two paints thoroughly combined. Continue adding paint and making swatches until your color becomes almost the same as the original hue of color #1. Do the same for your complementary color. These, then, are your tint scales for color #1 and its complement.

5. Toning a Color and its Complement with a Neutral Gray

Starting with color #1, put a portion of paint in a container. Paint a swatch. Then begin adding Neutral Gray 5 to your paint. After each addition, make two swatches of color. Continue working with this combination of paints until you feel paint #1 has been neutralized. Work in the same manner to obtain the color swatches for your complementary color. This group of colors is a second set of tones.

Notice the difference between these toned hues and the ones made by using a complementary color. Those

Blending of a color and its complement

Color (#1)
Slightly grayed color
Lightly grayed
Grayed color
Very grayed
Extremely grayed
Neutral blend
Extremely grayed
Very grayed
Grayed color
Lightly grayed
Slightly grayed color
Complementary color

Graying increases (top arrow, downward)

Graying increases (bottom arrow, upward)

Figure 10-4 Blending of a Color and its Complement
Place the pure color and its complement at opposite ends of the blending scale. Put the muddied middle-toned hue in the center. Place each root color's toned blends in order, moving from the least grayed at one end to the most grayed nearest the center.

made with the complementary color should be richer and more alive than those made with the neutral gray paint.

6. Making Color Scales with the Color Swatches

Make your own color scales using the hues from your different paint swatches to choose your graduated steps.

A. Make a value scale (include a total range of tints, pure hues, and shades) of both color #1 and its complement (figure 10-2).

B. Make tone scales for color #1 and its complement. For each scale, place the colors on the scale from the purest (most intense) to the grayest (figure 10-3).

C. Make a complementary scale by placing the color and its complement on opposite ends of the scale with the middle neutral color in the center (figure 10-4). Place hues on the scale in the appropriate color gradations, attempting to move in smooth steps.

Extended Learning:

EXTRA SUPPLIES: Leftover paint swatches from previous exercises, gluestick, scissors, template material, paper, pencil (for step #7)

Additional paint partners (for steps #8 and #9)

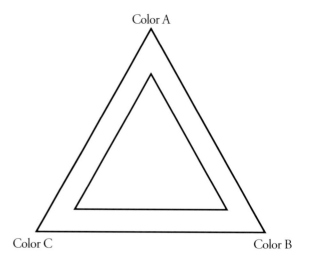

Figure 10-5 Triadic Color Triangle

7. Design Exercise Using Color Swatch Hues

Draw templates for a simple miniature traditional or contemporary design (at least 12 blocks). Using the paint swatches for your colors, cut up the pattern pieces. Then play with different color and value placements in the design. You should be able to create several designs out of your color swatches.

When placing the colors in a design, think about shapes, balance, direction, dominance, and proportion. Remember to create unity through both harmony and contrast. Do you have a focal point? How is your focal point emphasized?

When you play with your color swatches in your designs, think about the colors you are drawn to. Are they toned, tinted, shaded, or at full intensity?

8. Expanding Your Color Blending Experiences

If you would like to experiment with more paint combinations, choose other colors and their complements to work with. For each partnership make paint swatches as you did in the main section of this exercise. If you wish, make a value scale, a tone scale, and a complementary color scale. If you would like to work on design elements and principles of design with these new color combinations, use these swatches for your color and value changes in a design.

9. Triadic Color Blending

If you are particularly interested in using one of the triadic color schemes in a future design, choose the three color partners from one of these triadic sets (Chapter 4; photos 8A, B). As you have done previously, mix each combination of colors in two different color swatches and then continue adding paint. Begin with the pure hue combinations, blending each partner until their total mixture becomes an indistinct neutral hue. If you are using the secondary triad, you would blend three different partners: green with violet, violet with orange, and orange with green. Notice how the colors are beautifully muted when combined with their triadic partners.

Make a blending triangle to place selected colors from your gradated paint swatches (figure 10-5).

EXERCISE 3: BLENDING RELATED AND UNRELATED COLORS

OBJECTIVE: This exercise will begin by giving you experience working with simple related color blending. As you gain experience, you will achieve more difficult color blending with unrelated colors. This exercise should help you build a better understanding of color interaction and is a prerequisite for Exercise 4.

Supplies:

Letraset® Pantone Color Paper Selector Papers (Uncoated) (This is a set of 700 colors that comes in two packets. Each color is 2" x 4" in size and they may be found at art supply stores.) Note: Acrylic paints may be substituted for Pantone colors in this exercise.

Gluestick, drawing paper, colored pencils, scissors

NOTE: While doing these exercises, if you cannot conceptualize the blending of the hue partners, consider using a large set of colored pencils, watercolor pencils, or paint to use as blending tools. Either mix the two colors together with paint or pencil, or add one of the colors of paint or pencil to the colored paper partner. Blend the colors lightly so you can see how the hues interact with each other. This blend should give you enough of a clue to know what to look for in your Pantone papers.

Directions:

1. Blending Hues from the Same Color Family

Choose one color family (e.g., blue) that you would like to work with. On drawing paper, make 10 sets of 1½" x 2" rectangles. Divide these into three ½" rectangular strips (figure 10-6). Within each rectangular set, glue in place ½" x 2" color strips that fit the description of each of the following partners:

1 pure hue + pure hue	1 shade + shade
1 tint + tint	1 tone + tone
1 pure + 1 shade	1 pure + 1 tint
1 pure + 1 tone	1 shade + 1 tone
1 shade + 1 tint	1 tint + 1 tone

For each set, find a hue closest to the middle blend of the color partners. After a color has been chosen, cut out a rectangle of this hue to fit into the center space (make it a little wider than ½" so that no white space

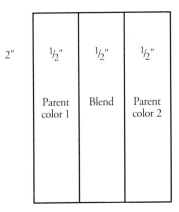

Figure 10-6 Blending Sets

shows). From a distance, each set of colors should blend together visually.

If you blend two pure hues, the middle color will also be pure. (Check the color wheel, photo 4, if you need help.) When you blend two tints together, and if they are from the same parent colors with only value differences, you only have to find the middle value to achieve an accurate blending. However, if the tints come from slightly different parents within the same relative color family, the center color will be a blend of both hue and value. The same holds true for blending two sets of shades and tones.

2. Blending Hues from Complementary Partners

Draw six sets of rectangles (figure 10-6). In each set, place the complementary partners on the outer divisions. In the center of each set, put a blend of each partner. This blend can be an average of both colors (toned, indistinct hue), or it can be a hue that leans more toward one of the partners. The complementary partners are:

yellow + violet	yellow-green + purple
green + magenta	blue-green + red
turquoise + orange	blue + yellow-orange

3. Blending Tint Complementary Colors

Choose tints of each complementary partner and place them on the outer sides of six new rectangular sets; find the blend for each set; place it in the center division.

4. Blending Shaded Complementary Colors

Find the blending hues that visually join the six shade combinations of the complementary partnerships. Place these color partners and their blended hues in six new rectangular sets.

5. Blending Toned Complementary Colors

Choose tones from each complementary partnership; place them in the outer sides of six more rectangular sets; find their blended counterparts and place them in the center of each set.

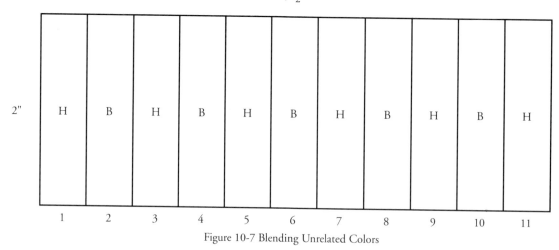
5½"

| H | B | H | B | H | B | H | B | H | B | H |

2"

1   2   3   4   5   6   7   8   9   10   11

Figure 10-7 Blending Unrelated Colors

6. Blending Unrelated Colors

Draw a rectangular column that is 5 ½" wide and 2" high. Divide the column into eleven ½" x 2" sections (figure 10-7). Number the sections from one to eleven.

Choose six unrelated colors from your Pantone set (or paints) to work with. Cut each color into strips ½" x 2." Position the colors in the odd-numbered sections marked H (hue). Place them in a random order. Glue the strip to the sections.

Try to find the hue that is the best blend of each odd-numbered pair. Each mixture should be placed between its two parent colors in the spaces marked B (blend). (Make certain the blended color is slightly larger than ½" so that no white shows from the background.) The blend of these two parent colors should be an average of the value, hue, and intensity (grayness). If you cannot find the exact middle hue, use one that comes closest to being an offspring of the parent colors. Glue down the first middle color on the first even-numbered space.

Work through the entire column, finding each pair's offspring. After you have glued in place the five offspring hues, look at your column from a distance. All the colors should visually blend into each other. If one offspring color attracts your attention more than any others, it will probably be an uneven blending of the two parents. Attempt to find a better blend, if possible.

7. Blending Unrelated Colors—Using Different Hues

Do the above exercise again, using different hues. Try to challenge yourself with more difficult color combinations during the second attempt. If you need help, use colored pencils or paints to give you clues to the offspring colors.

EXERCISE 4: WORKING WITH TRANSPARENCIES

OBJECTIVE: After working with this exercise, you should be better able to incorporate transparencies into your designs.

PREREQUISITE: Exercises 2 and 3

REFERENCES: Chapter 6

Supplies:

Letraset® Pantone Color Paper Selector Papers (Uncoated) (or acrylic paints) (*Same as exercise 3.*)
Paper, pencil, scissors, gluestick

Directions:

1. Both Colors Appear Transparent with a Backlit Background:

Draw six sets of triangles on paper similar to photo 13 or figure 10-8. Each triangular set should have an intersecting transparent area. Place each pair's transparent color in this blended area.

Select 6 pairs of the following color combinations:
    1 set of high-valued warm colors
    1 set of high-valued cool colors
    1 set of medium-valued warm colors
    1 set of medium-valued cool colors
    1 set of low-valued warm colors
    1 set of low-valued cool colors

Using triangular shapes, again find the offspring blend of the above parent colors. Glue the three colors in place.

For each set, find the offspring color closest to the midpoint of both parent colors in value and hue. If your two parent colors are similar in receding and advancing qualities, and if these colors are fairly similar in value, their offspring should give the illusion of both colors being transparent (photo 13A). Look at your transparency combinations from a distance. If they all look as if you can see through both colors into a backlit area, you have succeeded in attaining this type of transparency. If any have not acquired this look, attempt to find a better offspring color.

2. Creating a Filmy Transparency

Create a form of transparency that looks as if the top color is a transparent film over the lower color, which appears opaque. For this illusion, the offspring color will not be equal distance between the two parent colors in value or hue as in #1; instead, there will be differences in value, temperature, and intensity characteristics. However, these qualities will not be extreme (photos 13B and C).

Choose six color partnerships which include a variety of hues, values, and intensities. These color pairs should fit into the description provided above. Find a blending color that will be an offspring of both colors. However, rather than attempt to have it midpoint in value and hue, with similar temperature qualities, have the offspring color lean slightly toward one color in its tendencies, creating a filmy appearance. Cut colors to fit into triangular forms. Glue colors in place. Look at your color transparencies from a distance. They each should look as though a film has been cast over an opaquely colored object. If any of your combinations have not resulted in this effect, either change the intersecting color to make it more effective or replace one of the parent colors.

3. Floating Transparencies

If you would like to create the illusion of floating transparencies (photos 13D and E), choose six color combinations that seem to contrast highly in hue, value, and temperature (and perhaps intensity). Choose two offspring colors for each set. The first offspring color should have more qualities of one parent than the other. Select the second offspring to be more like the second parent color. Place the color sets into triangular shapes. Look at both transparency blendings from a distance. Notice how their slight changes affect the illusion.

Depending on the parent colors chosen, their individual characteristics, and which offspring color is decided on, the floating quality will range from near to far in distance. If the offspring most resembles the warmest parent hue, the cooler parent color will recede. How far it recedes will depend on the differences in value, hue, and temperature.

Combine many different combinations of color, value, intensity, and temperature to obtain a feel for how the colors blend and interact with each other.

EXERCISE 5: LUSTER

OBJECTIVE: This exercise will give you a better understanding of how to create the illusion of luster in a design.

REFERENCE: Chapter 5

Supplies:

Leftover paint swatches or colors from the Letraset®
    Pantone Color Paper Selectors (Uncoated)
    paper, pencil, scissors, and gluestick

Directions:

1. **Draw a rectangular band approximately 1 inch wide by 6 inches long (figure 10-9).**

    Sort through your color swatches in exercise #2 or 3. Pull out those swatches which give you a range of values in one coloration. You will need values that range from the gentlest tints to the darkest shades (they do not have to be in perfect gradations).

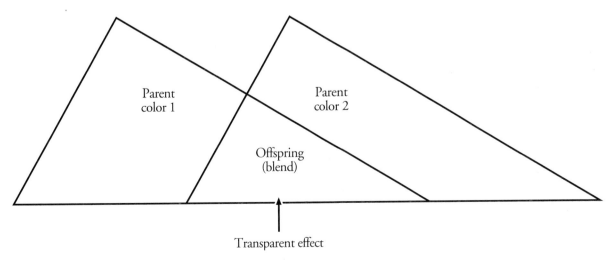

Figure 10-8 Blending Colors to Achieve Transparency

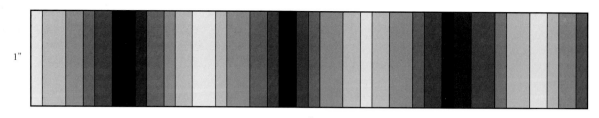

1"

6"

Figure 10-9 Lustrous Band
Use a range of graded values in a variety of widths to achieve luster.

Cut very narrow strips of value changes from the color swatches (⅛" to ¼"). Arrange them in order from medium to dark to medium to light to medium, having at least 8 to 12 value steps between each medium value. Continue repeating the pattern to fill in the whole band. Glue these strips onto your rectangular band. Then reverse their order, working from the darkest value back to the lightest. Repeat these value intervals as many times as you have space and colors. Look at your band from a distance. If it appears to be lustrous, you have succeeded in achieving the illusion. If a hue or value is so prevalent that it pulls out, change the hue or lessen the width of it. See photo 10 for example.

You may also make a lustrous design by starting with the darkest values and working toward the lightest within the color family; then reverse the order to obtain the complete lustrous effect.

2. Make another lustrous band using only toned hues.

Beginning with your highest valued tones, work with narrow strips until you reach your lowest values in the same color family. Then reverse the order.

If you would like to repeat another lustrous toned band, begin the interval with the darkest values and work toward the lightest tones. Notice the subtle design difference.

ACTIVITY 1:
IDENTIFYING YOUR PERSONAL COLOR PREFERENCES

OBJECTIVE: This activity is suggested to help identify your personal color preferences so that you can utilize these colors better in your surface designs.

Directions:

Using books, magazines, advertisements, calendars, photographs, and other printed matter, start collecting pictures for a color preference file. Anytime you see a picture that attracts your attention because of its coloring,

place it in the file. After you have collected colors for at least a year, you will find a definite pattern emerging from your choices. Use this knowledge to choose colors for your designs.

You may also find that one particular type of color scheme attracts you. This, too, is important information to know about yourself. Make a separate file folder for your color scheme preference, if you have a definite leaning toward one or two particular themes.

Over the years you may find that your color preferences change or grow toward more complex combinations. Keep track of these intuitive changes. They are important factors when designing.

ACTIVITY 2: PROMOTING INDIVIDUAL COLOR VISUALIZATION

OBJECTIVES: After establishing color files and studying the file pictures, you should better understand color scales, their visual differences, and each scale's unique characteristics and visual impact.

REFERENCES: Chapter 2

Directions:

Begin making color files that illustrate the four different color scales (Chapter 2). Using books, magazines, advertisements, calendars, photographs, and other printed matter, start collecting pictures to put in these file folders. Suggested file folder divisions include:

| spring | summer | autumn |
| winter | sunrise | night |

Study the file pictures to increase your understanding of color and how the scales differ. They also should be excellent illustrations of how to put colors together in a color scale. The examples you file should give you impressions, subtle clues, or obvious examples of the color scales, their hues, and their emotive impact. Use these examples for guidelines when you begin creating your own designs.

ACTIVITY 3: PROMOTING UNDERSTANDING OF ILLUSIONS

OBJECTIVES: After you establish these files and study the pictures that go into each folder, you should better understand the various illusions and their individual characteristics. You should also be able to distinguish the necessary color requirements of each, so that you can incorporate a specific illusion into a design with little difficulty.

REFERENCES: Chapters 5 and 6

Directions:

Begin organizing file folders which include examples of color illusions. Collect these samples from magazines, books, calendars, cards, and other printed materials. Use these color cues for references when planning your own designs that include one or more illusions. Study the illusions carefully. Observe the close changes in hue that effectively create the specific illusion.

Your file folder divisions may include:

luminosity	luster
shadows	transparency
iridescence	opalescence
auroras	linear movement
color movement	depth
reflections	mist
atmospheric perspective	other illusions
highlights	

"Research in painting means nothing. Finding is what counts . . . If a man finds something—anything—even if that was not his intention, he will at least excite our curiosity if not our admiration. When I paint, I try to show what I have found, not what I am looking for. In art, intentions are not enough. What counts is what one does, not what one intends to do. Everyone knows that art is not truth. Art is a lie that makes us realize truth, or at least the truth we are given to understand."

"A beginner should look at his subject, the reality he wants to reproduce, through a filter that virtually lets only one color through with all its more or less light, more or less luminous tones.'

—Pablo Picasso,
Spanish painter and sculptor,
1881–1973
Drawing With Color and Imagination

"Don't proceed according to rules and principles, but paint what you observe . . . Paint generously and unhesitatingly, for it is best not to lose the first impression."

—Camille Pissarro
French painter, 1830–1903
The Impressionists

CHAPTER 11

Patterns

The following five traditional patterns have been innovatively used by quilt artists whose work is included in The Gallery. Consider making your own creative interpretations of these traditional designs in a future quilt. Creatively use colors and values to achieve the desired effects. If necessary, adapt the designs to your own needs by adding, deleting, or moving lines or sections of the block pattern. All patterns included in this section can be easily drafted to any size by using the basic drafting instructions in Appendix II.

11-1. RAIL FENCE

The most beautiful quilt in print created using the Rail Fence design is "Gradation" (photo 84) by Regula Nussbaumer of Switzerland. Regula has effectively moved the analogous colors through the quilt with this block's simple design elements.

Below is the traditional fabric setting for Rail Fence, using only four fabrics. Rather than following the traditional plan, attempt to create an innovative design from Rail Fence blocks that moves colors and values through the total design. To do this, use a large selection of fabrics (figures 11-1 A, B).

11-2. PINWHEEL, DOUBLE PINWHEEL (TURNSTILE), BIG DIPPER, AND YANKEE PUZZLE

The Pinwheel, Double Pinwheel, Big Dipper, and Yankee Puzzle designs are some of the simplest blocks, technically, to construct. They are all related to four-patch designs. Four quilts in The Gallery are examples of extraordinarily different results from these traditional designs.

"Ancient Directions" (photo 18) by Alison Goss uses a variation of Double Pinwheel (Turnstile) for her major design component. Her fabric use and manipulation of the block setting and its size to create the effect of depth give spellbinding results.

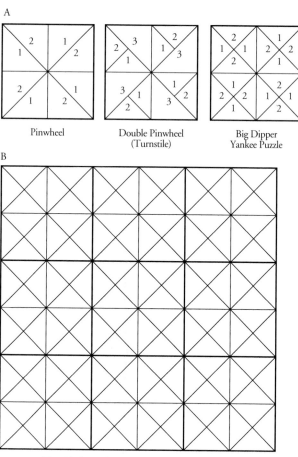

Pinwheel   Double Pinwheel (Turnstile)   Big Dipper Yankee Puzzle

Nine-block grid for designing pinwheel coloration.

Figure 11-2 Pinwheel, Double Pinwheel, Big Dipper, Yankee Puzzle (four-patch design)

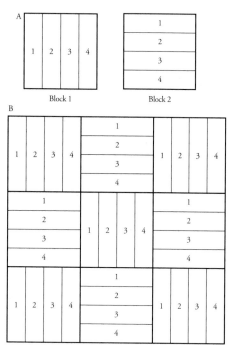

Figure 11-1 Rail Fence

Judith Tinkl's "Autumn" (photo 24) uses a variation of the Pinwheel or Yankee Puzzle pattern with amazing results. Her color application illustrates one of the most innovative uses of this traditional pattern. "Scintillation" and "Dancing Twilight" (photos 82, 86) are variations of the Pinwheel or Big Dipper pattern. However, the center of the block pattern was drawn slightly off center to give the illusion of curving motion when several blocks are set together. These two designs are created from the exact same design; achieving two extremely different designs from the same pattern illustrates the profound importance color can play in an artwork.

These simple traditional patterns contain endless possibilities when you apply your imagnation to changing colors, values, sizes, and settings within the overall design. The varied applications pictured here should give you ideas to begin your own fascinating, and perhaps complex, color exploration using these uncomplicated triangular designs.

The traditional fabric placements of these triangular patterns are shown here. Draft several block designs. Then experiment with color placements on a paper plan by numbering the triangular pieces within the design *or* by drawing triangular pieces directly on flannel and then working extemporaneously on the flannel (figures 11-2 A, B).

11-3. SPIDERWEB

"Opals in the Web" (photo 49) by Pat Magaret is a variation of the classic Spiderweb pattern, an eight-pointed star design. Pat has made her own fabric for the different web sections by sewing strips of fabric together.

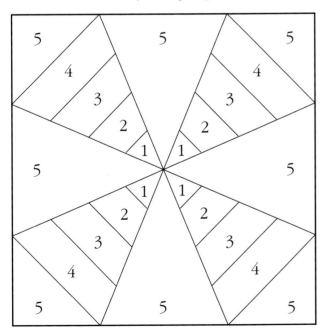

Figure 11-3 Spiderweb (eight-pointed star design)

These have been placed together in random order to give the flickering effect of opalescent colors.

The design and illusionary potential of Spiderweb is almost limitless with this traditional design. It is an excellent pattern in which to attempt to create movement, luster, luminosity, and transparency by color and value manipulation.

One of the traditional fabric placements for this traditional pattern is shown below. Interesting new patterns can be created by dividing the background triangles into smaller sections and using color and value changes across the total design. The minimum number of blocks required to achieve a good design is nine.

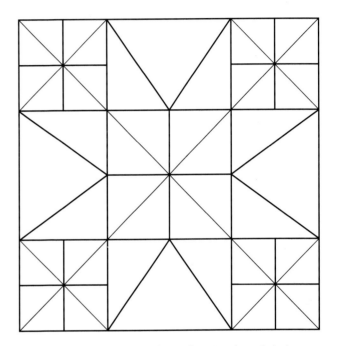

Figure 11-4 54-40 or Fight (eight-pointed star design)

11-4. 54–40 OR FIGHT

A variation of a popular traditional pattern has been used by Nancy Breland to create her lovely quilt "First Light" (photo 62). This design is drafted from eight-pointed star design markings. Nancy has not divided the center square of the star in her quilt, as seen in many traditional quilts made from this pattern. Instead, she has used larger pieces of fabrics for her star centers.

Figure 11-4 is one of the traditional design variations for this pattern. This is a wonderful design to use when you want to experiment with value changes in the background because of the small background squares. Consider using a large selection of fabrics to attain your color and value changes.

11-5. Storm at Sea

Storm at Sea has been one of the most popular traditional patterns through the years. It is a four-patch design that needs a 64-square grid (8 x 8) to attain all the design points. The variation created by Sarah Dickson and Maureen McGee (photo 69) is innovative in its color, design, and fabric use, allowing for all elements to move beyond the individual blocks. They also have eliminated part of the block design that repeats itself when placed with other blocks. This design change allows stars to move through the quilt design.

When you create your own Storm at Sea quilt, explore the possibilities of using the entire surface of the quilt to emphasize the design movement through changes in color and values.

A traditional Storm at Sea fabric assignment is shown below. Consider changing the plan to create a spectacular new design by using a completely different fabric plan. You can even change lines or delete entire sections of the block to change the design even more. Nine blocks are the minimum number to create an interesting design.

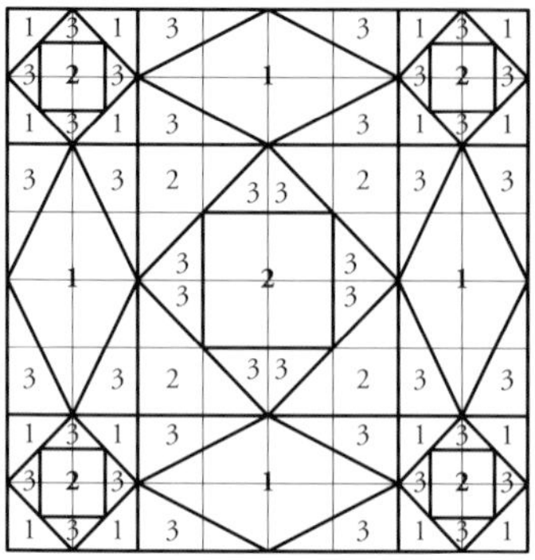

Figure 11-5A Storm at Sea
A Single Block (four-patch design; 64-square grid)

Figure 11-5B Storm at Sea
A Design in Nine Blocks

MORE DESIGNS TO ACHIEVE MAGICAL ILLUSIONARY EFFECTS

The five patterns that follow are either traditional designs, traditional design variations, or original traditional designs. Each of these block designs can be easily drafted to any size by using the basic instructions in Appendix II.

11-6. NORTH DAKOTA

North Dakota is a wonderful traditional pattern that can be used to emphasize color movement, transparency, the illusion of curves, and depth. This is a good design for using a multitude of fabrics from two different color families—or two different color temperatures.

A

Figure 11-6A North Dakota
A Single Block (four-patch design; 64-square grid)

Figure 11-6B North Dakota
A Design in Nine Blocks

B

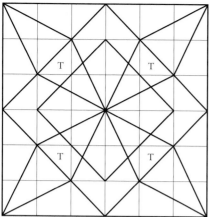

T = Transparency

11-7. BARBARA BANNISTER'S TRANSPARENT STAR (VARIATION JW 1992)

This variation of Barbara Bannister's Star has been designed to allow for transparency between the two major design components—the four-pointed star and the open squares. With planning, there can be three levels of depth: the background, the squares, and the stars. To add beauty and intrigue, use all three types of transparency so that the floating capabilities of the stars and squares are transposed in the design.

Figure 11-7A Barbara Bannister's Transparent Star—A Single Block
(nine-patch design; 36-square grid) by Joen Wolfrom, 1992—Pattern variation of Barbara Bannister's Star
Figure 11-7B Barbara Bannister's Transparent Star—A Design in Nine Blocks

11-8. GLOWING STARS AND GEMS

Glowing Stars and Gems, an original design (JW 1992), is a five-patch design that can be used to create several illusions by color, value, and fabric manipulation. Depth, shading, and highlights can be incorporated in the star lattice. The gem stars can be created with depth, luminosity, and luster. Glowing Stars and Gems has been designed so that one block flows into another, forming a lovely, overall pattern. Color gradations in the background areas can flow from one design element to another. You may also wish to use your knowledge that warm colors advance and cool colors recede in choosing colors for this design. Nine blocks is the minimum number of blocks needed to create an effective design.

The block design has been broken into numbered pattern pieces to show one possible color and value application. Feel free to make their placement choices to fit your design goals.

Figure 11-8A Glowing Gems and Stars—Basic Design (5-patch design; 100-square design) designed by Joen Wolfrom, 1992
Figure 11-8B A Suggested Color Application,
Figure 11-8C Glowing Stars—A Design in Nine Blocks

11-9. BLOOMING LATTICE

Blooming Lattice is an original variation (JW 1992) of the four-patch pattern Lena's Choice. It is designed with spring in mind, with a star flower set against the green of vegetation and the blue sky beyond. The lattice adds another design dimension. By shifting the colors slightly, the lattice can play a more prominent role; or the greenery can be increased. Naturally, the star flowers can be made in a variety of blooming colors. If you create a quilt using this design, use many different fabrics for each design feature rather than one or two. By using a multitude of fabrics you will create interesting color intermingling and more vibrancy.

Figure 11-9A Blooming Lattice—Basic Design (four-patch design; 64-square grid) designed by Joen Wolfrom—A deriviative of Lena's Choice
Figure 11-9B A Suggested Color Application, Figure 11-9C Blooming Lattice—A Design in Nine Blocks

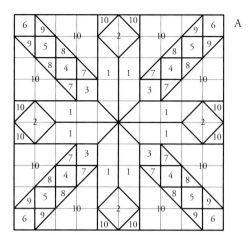

11-10. CROSSING PATHS

Crossing Paths is an original design (JW 1992) that stems from the traditional pattern Century of Progress. It is designed so that the stars can appear three-dimensional. These stars can also show shadows or highlights. The pathway behind the stars can be made using color or value gradations. The background area can achieve mistiness or the illusion of far distance by the use of toned fabrics. For best results, the background should be broken into small areas of varied fabric placement to allow the colors to mingle.

Figure 11-10A Crossing Paths—A Basic Design (five-patch design; 100-square grid) designed by Joen Wolfrom, 1992
Figure 11-10B Crossing Paths—A Design in Nine Blocks

In Conclusion

It is my hope that you realize you are a unique person whose own individual creativity lies deep within you, waiting to be released into conscious thought and artistic expression.

May this book offer you new ways of thinking about your own talents, how to put colors and designs together, and how to challenge your talents with illusionary ideas.

As you begin this journey into color and illusions, realize that when you work toward your creative potential, you must accept not being in complete control. Artwork has a mind of its own, forcing you to submit to its desires. Most importantly, however, you must accept that in any creative endeavor, you will be presented with many unknowns and risks. Each new idea or discovery you develop along the way will be as a direct result of a mistake made or an unexpected outcome, rather than from any prearranged plan made by you. Be willing to risk and then enjoy the benefits from these diversions.

Always keep in mind that the joy of creating art is not in its safety nor in its perfection, but in the challenges of successfully working through one's ideas and images . . . and growing with the experience.

Be particularly proud of your artistic accomplishments, as they are a unique expression of your inner self—the most priceless, remarkable gift you can give the world. May you continue to read, grow, risk, challenge, and explore. And, may designing and creating beautiful quilts and wall art always be a joy!

Joen

"The smallest goal achieved stands taller than the grandest intention.
Do whatever your heart leads you to do—but do it."

—Writer unknown

73. Dreaming of . . . A Room of My Own, 1991, 80" x 94"

Joen Wolfrom, Fox Island, Washington

An impressionistic view from an open window. Scene of Puget Sound, the Olympic Mountain Range, sunset, and hanging wisteria created using strip piecing techniques; open window and sill were hand appliquéd; wallpaper was traditionally pieced. Photo: Ken Wagner.

74

75

74. Rocky Mountain Vista, Frieze #7, 1989, 6' x 3'
Joy Nixon, Calgary, Alberta, Canada
Pieced and appliquéd scene; one of eight sections spanning forty feet. Traditional Attic Window is a wonderful foreground design. Split-complementary color scheme used. Owner: Sundre Hotel, Sundre, Alberta. Photo: John Dean.

75. Blue Horizon, 1992, 72" x 72"
Jason Yenter, Seattle, Washington
Strong design with intricate color and value changes. Split-complementary scheme used, with warm complement used as an accent. Photo: Ken Wagner.

76. Desert Wings, 1991, 60" x 96"
Jason Yenter, Seattle, Washington
Beautiful blend of colors creates this exquisite, strong, original design. Split-complementary color scheme is used with subtle hints of warmth intermingled with cool colors. Photo: Ken Wagner.

77. Rain, 1991, 80" x 31"
Karen Perrine, Tacoma, Washington
The complementary accent gives the illusion that light is hitting rain as it is falling. Wonderful illusion of water movement. Photo: Karen Perrine.

76

77

78. Blue Study, 1986, 48" x 48"
Patty Bentley, Newberg, Oregon
Toned hues and value changes create a subtle illusion of depth.
Private owner. Photo: Ed Dull.

79. Stories Grandpa Told Me, 1991, 76" x 76"
Cheryl Phillips, Pueblo, Colorado
Lovely original-designed traditional quilt showing transparency through
color blends. Central focal point design. Intricate quilting enhances the
design. Private owner. Photo: Ken Wagner.

80. Alpenglow, 1991, 57" x 74"
Carol Ann Wadley, Hillsboro, Oregon
A beautiful landscape created entirely from triangles and squares.
Excellent fabric selection enhances color and value changes.
Photo: Bill Bachhuber.

81. Out of Darkness, 1989, 137cm. x 148cm.
Katherine Picot, Bohl, Germany
Lovely effect created from color and value changes, using triangles and
squares. Photo: Franz Silzner Grafic Design & Fotografie.

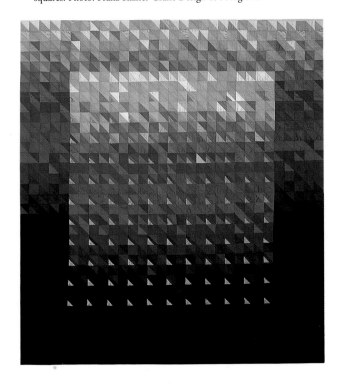

82

83

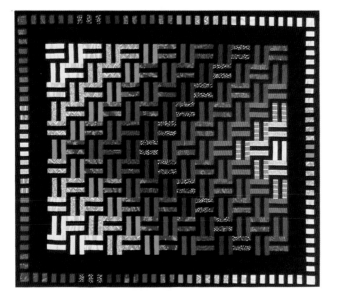

84

82. Scintillation, 1984, 63" x 35"
Joen Wolfrom, Fox Island, Washington
An abstract design color/value study, using a skewed version of the traditional Pinwheel pattern as a beginning point. Color movement is achieved by moving the colors across the surface of the design.
Owner: Catherine Smith. Photo: Ken Wagner.

83. Weaving, 1990, 16" x 16"
Pat Magaret, Pullman, Washington
A breathtaking color study creating the perception of luster, depth, and motion. Photo: Ken Wagner.

84. Gradation, 1989, 162cm x 142cm
Regula Nussbaumer, Eugelburg, Switzerland
Color flows through design, achieving a beautiful effect. A spectacular quilt created from the traditional Rail Fence design. An analogous color scheme is used. Border is innovative and enhances the design.
Private owner. Photo: Gross.

85. Fortissimo in Plum, 1985, 60" x 36"
Joen Wolfrom, Fox Island, Washington
Curves on the Whole design created with illusions of transparency and luminosity through color manipulation. Photo: Ken Wagner.

86. Dancing Twilight, 1984, 30" x 36"
Joen Wolfrom, Fox Island, Washington
Identical Pinwheel block design as in photo #82. Monochromatic color scheme gives design a different look. A good example of transparency.
Private owner. Photo: Ken Wagner.

85

86

APPENDIX I:

Linear Perspective

LINEAR PERSPECTIVE VOCABULARY

Picture Plane:

When you work in the two-dimensional perspective of width and height, the area of the design is considered the surface. When the third dimension, depth, is added, the surface of the artwork becomes the *picture plane*. The edges of the picture plane are actually the edges of your artwork (figure AI-1).

Ground Plane:

The *ground plane* is the (ground) area that lies between the bottom edge of the picture plane and the horizon line (figure AI-1).

Horizon Line:

The *horizon line* is the dividing line between the sky and the earth's surface, whether land or sea. It is always a horizontal line that lies parallel to the ground plane. The horizon line is always at the viewer's eye level, regardless of whether it can be seen or not.

The horizon line can be positioned any place in the picture plane. If the foreground is the focus point, the horizon line will be high. If the sky area is of prime importance, the horizon line will be placed at a low level. If neither is specifically stressed, the position of the horizon line will probably be somewhere within the middle third of the picture plane—preferably not dividing the picture plane in half, however (figure AI-1).

Vanishing Point:

The *vanishing point* is a point on the horizon line where all extended parallel lines in the ground plane meet. The vanishing point is the most important mark on the horizon line, as the perspective is based on this position. Depending on what you wish to draw, you may have one, two, or even more vanishing points along your horizon line.

Vanishing points along a horizon line can often be seen in our lives, such as down city streets or rows of plowed farm fields. As these objects recede in the distance, they appear to meet at the same point along the horizon line—the vanishing point (figure AI-1).

DETERMINING THE TYPE OF LINEAR PERSPECTIVE TO USE

The two main types of linear perspective are *one-point* and *two-point perspective*. In a landscape, use one-point perspective (also called parallel perspective) when you want extended parallel lines to appear as if they are receding into the distance. Use one-point perspective to draw two or three sides of a box if its front side lies parallel and perpendicular to the picture plane (figure AI-2).

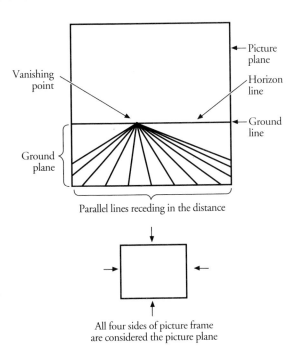

Figure AI-1 Linear Perspective Vocabulary
All four sides of picture frame are considered the picture plane.

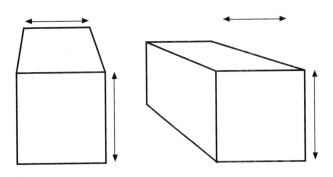

Figure AI-2 One-point Perspective

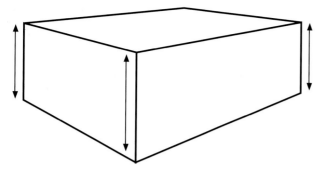

Figure AI-3 Two-point Perspective

In two-point perspective, the two viewed sides recede into the background from the front corner line—the height line. The top and bottom edges of the box are determined by extending lines from the top and bottom of the height line to the two vanishing points. Use two-point perspective for creating a box (or form) with two or three sides showing when the box's height lines are the only ones that lie parallel to the picture plane (figure AI-3).

One–point Perspective (Parallel Perspective)

1. Beginning Steps (figure AI-4): To begin, draw a picture plane. Draw the front side of your box where you want it placed in the picture plane. Next, lightly draw a horizon line extending from one side of the picture plane to the other. Place the vanishing point on this line. Determine its placement by the approximate angle you wish your box's sides to be.

2. Finding the Second Side (figure AI-5): Draw two lines from the upper square corners (A and B) to the vanishing point (C). These new lines will become the top's side edges. Determine how far into the distance you want the box's top to recede; place a dot on each

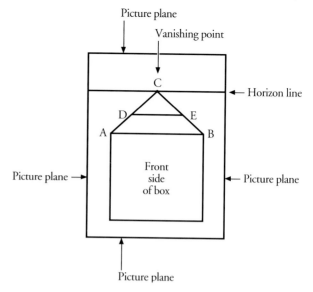

Figure AI-5 Finding the Second Side

side edge at exactly that distance (D and E); these dots will be the back corner edges of the box's top. Draw a line (DE) to create the box's back side. Erase all excess lines that are not needed (figure AI-5).

3. Marking the Inside: If you want to make the box appear to be open in the front, do the following: Draw lines from the box's front bottom corners (F and G) to the vanishing point (C). These lines (FC and GC) establish the bottom side edges of the box. To determine the back corners, draw vertical lines from the back top corners (D and E) to the angled bottom side lines (FC and GC). These vertical lines must be perpendicular (90 degrees) to the top back edge line (DE). The box's inside bottom edge is made by drawing a horizontal line connecting the two back corners (HJ) (figure AI–6).

4. Floating Boxes: To see the underneath side of the box, place the horizon line and vanishing point below the front of the box in the picture plane. Then obtain the bottom side and back edges by following the same procedures as in #2 and 3. This gives the illusion of a floating box (figure AI-7).

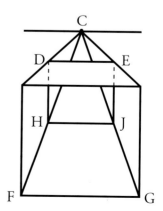

Figure AI-6 Marking the Insides

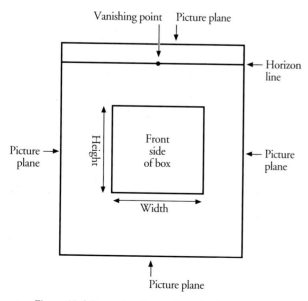

Figure AI-4 One-point Perspective—Beginning Steps

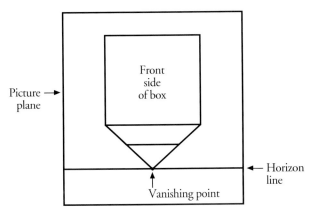

Figure AI-7 Floating Box

5. Creating Designs Using Clusters of Boxes: You can create interesting designs by using one-point perspective. Draw the box fronts as you want them positioned in the picture plane. Then determine the placement of the vanishing point and horizon line according to the design you want. Buildings or boxes set on a ground plane work quite well with clustering forms (A). You may even consider "playing" with the rules a bit to achieve innovative possibilities, creating interesting perspective designs (B) (figures AI-8A and B).

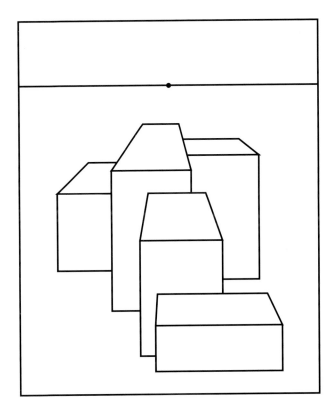

Figure AI-8A Creating Designs
Using Clusters of Boxes—Formal Setting

Figure AI-8B Creating Designs Using Clusters of Boxes—Innovative Setting

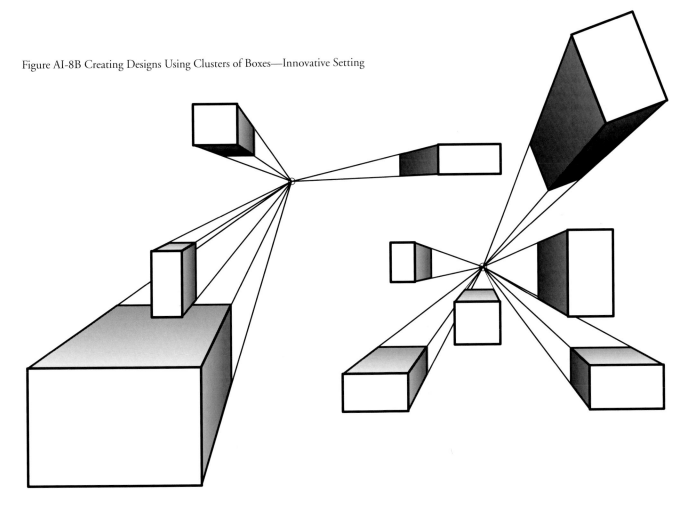

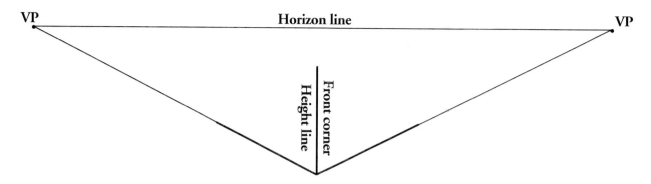

Figure AI-9 Two-Point Perspective—Establishing the Vanishing Points

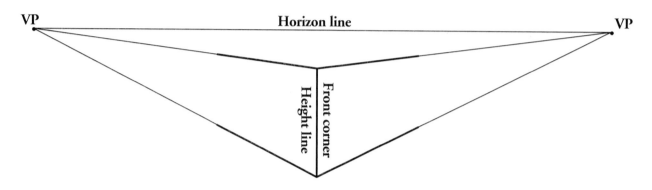

Figure AI-10 Drawing the Right and Left Top Edges

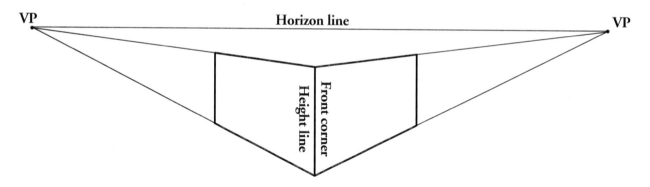

Figure AI-11 Drawing the Vertical Back Corners

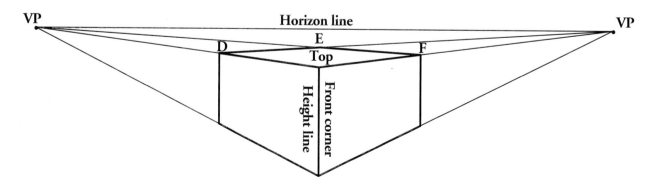

Figure AI-12 Drawing the Top Back Lines

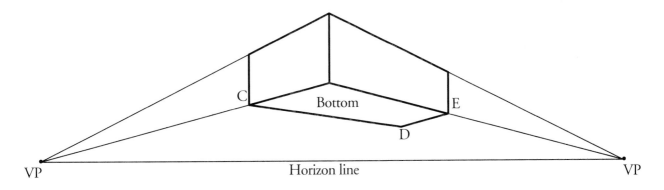

Figure AI-13 Drawing the Bottom Back Lines

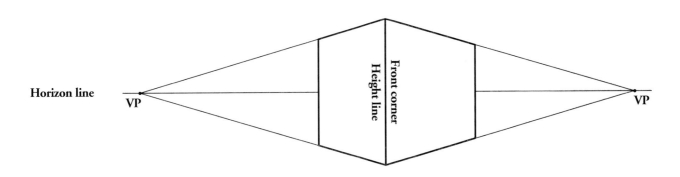

Figure AI-14 Drawing a Two-sided Box

Two–point Perspective

6. Beginning Steps: Draw the picture plane. Determine where the box is to be placed in the picture plane. Determine how tall the box's sides are to be; draw the height line (front corner).

7. Establishing the Vanishing Points: Visualize the desired angle of the box's bottom edges. Lightly sketch these angles. Then, at the bottom point of the height line, accurately draw extended lines on the right and left sides, using your sketched angle as a guide. Draw the horizon line which intersects the two extended lines and is perpendicular to the height line. The points where the lines intersect are the vanishing points (figure AI–9).

Next, establish the box's right and left top edges by drawing lines from the top of the height line to the vanishing points (figure AI-10).

8. Drawing the Vertical Back Corners: Determine how far you want the left side to recede into the distance (by eye or measurement) and mark a dot on the bottom line at that point. This mark is the bottom corner point. Draw a line from this point to the top edge extended line. This line will be the back left vertical edge. It must be parallel to the front corner

line. Repeat this process for the right back vertical corner (figure AI-11).

9. Drawing the Top Back Lines: To make the top back edges, draw a line from the upper back right corner (F) to the left vanishing point. Then draw a line from the upper back left corner (D) to the right vanishing point. The intersection of those two lines creates the farthest back corner (E) (figure AI-12).

10. Drawing the Bottom Back Lines: To create a box that appears to float, adjust the side angles so that the vanishing point and horizon line lie below the height line (corner line). Then proceed to draw side and bottom edges in the same manner as those drawn with the horizon line above the height line (figure AI-13).

Strategy Note: If you want the top of the box to be seen, the vanishing points and horizon line lie above the height line or front corner (see figure AI-12). If the bottom of the box is to be seen, the vanishing points and horizon line lie below the height line (see figure AI-13). If only two sides of the box are to be seen, the horizon line is positioned so that it intersects the height line; the vanishing points are positioned at either end (figure AI-14).

11. Creating Innovative Designs: You may create innovative designs with several boxes in your picture plane. The simplest design using a cluster of boxes is one that uses the same horizon line and vanishing points for all. Visualize where you want the different boxes to be placed; draw height lines in each designated area. Then establish the horizon line and vanishing points. As in the methods used above, draw the lines for each box, one at a time. The boxes can differ by varying the length of the height lines and the box sides. Also, choosing to place boxes below, above, and on the horizon line will create differences (figure AI-15).

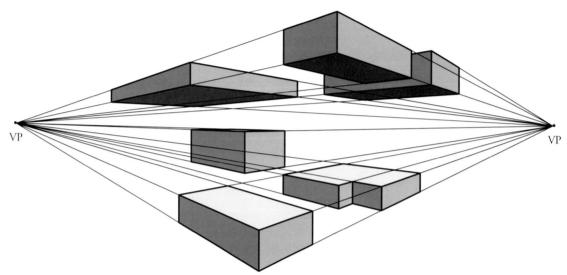

Figure AI-15 Creating Innovative Designs with Two-point Perspective

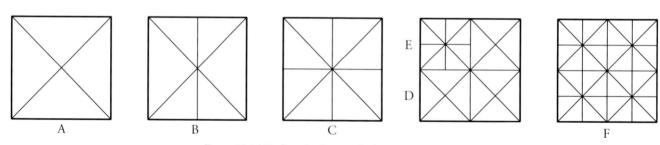

Figure AI-16 Finding the Center of a Square or Rectangle

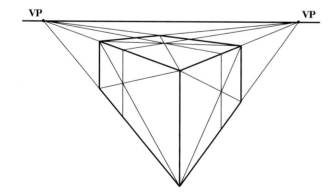

Figure AI-17 Drawing the Grid on a Box

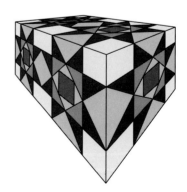

Figure AI-18 Drawing a Design on the Sides of a Box

Putting a Design on the Side of a Box

There may be times when you wish to create a surface design that incorporates traditional block designs on boxes or other objects that have been done in perspective. For instance, it is fun to include a patchwork design on the sides of a box (photo 27). Use the following method to create any patchwork design in which the pattern grid is divisible by two.

12. Finding the Center of a Square or Rectangle: Draw a square or rectangle. Draw diagonal lines from corner to corner (A). The center point, no matter what four-sided configuration you draw, is located where the two lines intersect. The square can be divided in half again by drawing vertical and horizontal lines through the intersection (B and C). Each of the quarters of a square can be halved by drawing diagonal lines that intersect the first diagonal lines (D).

    With these intersecting diagonals, each quandrant can be broken into four small squares (E). This results in the square being broken into 16 squares. These small squares can be divided further by adding more diagonal lines. Thus, by dividing each quadrant into 16 tiny squares, this square can be easily divided into 64 square divisions without having to use a calculator or measuring tool (figure AI-16, A-F).

13. Drawing the Grid on a Box: By using the above method to draw your grid lines, you can easily design a 4-patch design to go on the sides of a box.

First, decide which 4-patch design you want to use; determine how many grid squares you need to draw the design on the box (8, 16, 64). Draw the box in perspective using either one-point or two-point perspective.

Begin making the grid, drawing diagonal lines from corner to corner to find the midpoint and then drawing horizontal and vertical lines going through the center. Continue in this manner, dividing the square into equal divisions, until you have formed the number of squares you need to obtain the grid (figure AI-17).

14. Drawing the Design on the Box Sides: Once you have the grid in place, draw the design on the box sides. Draw the design lines on the grid. It should be easy to follow the pattern lines if you have made your grid lines accurately. Use the lines and intersecting points as guides to drawing the design. You may place as many blocks as you want on your box sides. If you want, you may also put the design on the top or bottom of the box (figure AI-18).

15. Other Divisions: If you want to create a traditional design on a box that is divisible by three, five, or seven units, you need to use another method of dividing the square into equal divisions. See Appendix II for pattern drafting instructions for nine-patch, five-patch and seven-patch designs.

"Where the one sees only the external outline of objects, the other—the Impressionist—sees the living lines, not put together geometrically but in a thousand irregular strokes which, seen at a distance, establish life. Where the one sees things placed in perspective planes, according to a theoretical design, the other—the Impressionist again—sees perspective conveyed by a thousand little touches of tone and brush, and by all kinds of atmospheric states."

—Jules Laforgue
French writer and poet, 1860–1887
writing about Impressionists.
The Impressionists

First Steps in Pattern Drafting

So many beautiful traditional patterns have been designed throughout the generations. We only see a small number of these designs actually put into quilts because many people do not know how to pattern draft; most of these patterns are not readily available in commercial patterns. When you know how to pattern draft, you have the freedom to choose any design and draw it to the exact size you want—even to a fraction of an inch. Knowing how to pattern draft eliminates the need to buy commercial patterns. The basic pattern drafting techniques for grid designs and eight-pointed star designs, two of the most common types of traditional designs, are included here.

GRID DESIGNS

The majority of quilts are made from gridded block designs: four-patch, nine-patch, five-patch, and seven-

patch. Four-patch designs can be divided into 4, 16, or 64 divisions in the block (A). These divisions are divided into squares making up a grid. Nine-patch designs are divided into 9 or 36 squares in the grid (B); five-patch designs are made with 25 divisions in the grid (C); and seven-patch designs are divided into a grid of 49 squares (D).

It is easiest to draft patterns on plain paper instead of graph paper because the graph lines can be confusing. Tools needed for drafting are a pencil, 24-inch ruler, and a 12-inch colored drafting triangle. No calculator is needed with this method. Follow these instructions:

1. Draw an Accurate Square to Create the Block

A. Drawing a Base Line. Draw a base line, starting with point A and ending with point B (figure AII-1). Points A and B will be the bottom corner points of your square. Line A-B should be the exact measurement of the block you want (i.e., line A-B is 11 inches long for an 11-inch block).

B. Drawing the Left Vertical Side. With drafting triangle, draw the left vertical side of the square by placing the bottom of your triangle on the base line, with the 90-degree corner at point A. Draw a vertical line slightly longer than you need. With ruler, mark a dot at the 11-inch mark (or your desired length of line) on line A-C.

C. Drawing the Right Vertical Side. With drafting triangle, draw the right vertical side of the square by placing the bottom of the triangle on the base line, with the 90-degree corner at point B. Draw a vertical line slightly longer than needed. With ruler, mark a dot at the 11-inch mark (or your desired length of line) on line B-D.

D. Drawing the Top Side. Place the drafting triangle on line B-D with the 90-degree corner placed on point D. Draw the fourth side of the square by drawing a line from point D to point C. (You may also place the drafting triangle on line A-C and point D to draw the fourth side.)

E. Finishing the Square. After the four sides have been drawn, check to see that the square has been accurately drawn. Place the drafting triangle at each corner

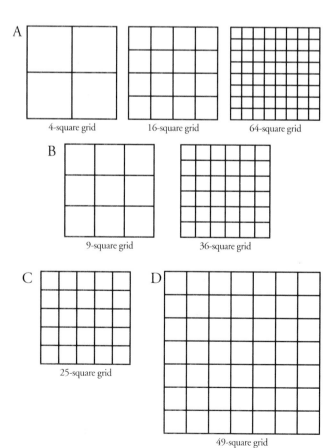

of the square. If the square's corner matches the drafting triangle's 90-degree corner, the square is accurate. If it doesn't match, correct the problem.

2. Form the Grid

Once you have drawn the square, look closely at the design you have chosen. Determine how many divisions are needed horizontally and vertically (e.g., 2, 4, 8, 5, 7, 6, 9) to recreate the design in the square. If the design is a four-patch pattern needing a grid of 64 squares (for example, see figure F, Stars and Squares traditional block pattern), the block must be divided into eight equal divisions horizontally and vertically. To create this grid do the following:

A. Determine the Incremental Measurement. Ask yourself what is the lowest number that is larger than eleven (size of square) and can be divided evenly by eight (the number of divisions needed). (The answer is sixteen.) Determine how many times eight goes into sixteen. Eight will go into sixteen two times ($16 \div 8 = 2$).

B. Make the Grid Markings. Place the ruler at 0 point at corner A on the 11-inch square. Place the 16-inch mark of the ruler on the opposite vertical line (BD). Mark with a small dot every 2 inches along the ruler from 0 to 16 inches (8 divided into 16 inches equals 2 inches; figure AII-2).

C. Drawing the First Grid Lines. Place the drafting triangle on the base line, lining it up to the first dot. Using the base line and dot as reference points, draw a vertical line from the bottom of the square to its top. Draw vertical lines at each dot (figure AII-3).

D. Finishing the Grid. Move your paper one quarter turn so that line C-A is at the bottom of the page directly in front of you. Place the ruler at point 0 on corner C. Place the 16-inch mark at the opposite vertical line A-B. Mark every 2 inches along the ruler, as done previously. With the drafting triangle placed on line CA and the dots as reference points, draw vertical lines at each marking (figure AII-4). When you have completed lines at 2-, 4-, 6-, 8-, 10-, 12-, and 14-inch markings, you will have made a 64-square grid. Now draw any 64-square design on your gridded square.

E. A Variation in Drafting: Extending the Line. Sometimes the square's lines (DB and AB) are too short for the ruler positioning. It is then necessary to extend those two vertical lines in order to position the ruler accurately. This extension is particularly necessary when a large number of divisions are needed in a relatively small square (figure AII-5).

For instance, if you have a 10-inch square and want to divide it into 6 divisions, the ruler's 12-inch mark

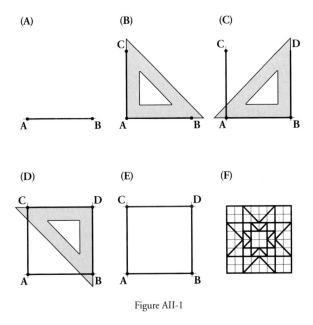

Figure AII-1

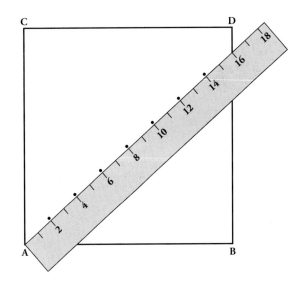

Figure AII-2

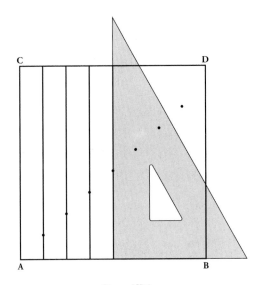

Figure AII-3

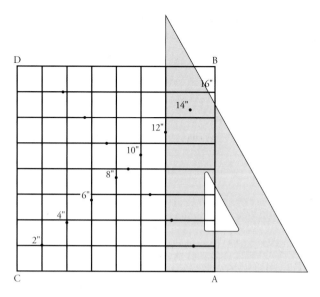

Figure AII-4

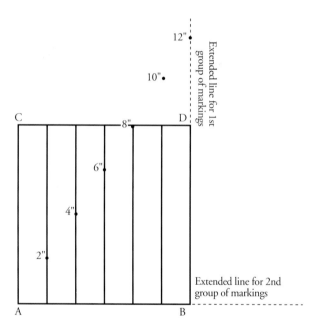

Figure AII-5

must be placed on line BD (12 is the first number larger than 10 that is divisible by 6). If you place the ruler at the 0 point at square's corner A, you will see that the 12-inch marking on the ruler does not lie on line BD in the square. Therefore, line BD needs to be extended several inches past the edge of the corner.

After the line has been extended, place the 12-inch mark of the ruler on the extended BD line while the 0 mark is on corner A. Then make the needed marks; draw the vertical lines. Next, extend line AB to make the second set of marks to finish the grid lines.

3. Making Your Design on the Gridded Square

Use the grid lines to redraw the design you have chosen to make. (See example, Stars and Squares traditional block.) Consider changing, adding, or deleting lines in the pattern if you think it will enhance the design. Trace the lines of the most accurately-drawn elements for your templates on plastic or other sturdy material. See Chapter 11 for several patterns that can be drafted in the grid method described.

DRAFTING EIGHT-POINTED STARS

There are many beautiful eight-pointed star designs available. Although they look similar to nine-patch designs, they are not the same, and must be drafted in a different manner. In a nine-patch design, the three major divisions are equal in size. In an eight-pointed star design, although the square is divided into thirds, the middle division is larger than the other two. Besides the usual drafting tools, a compass is needed. Follow these directions to create beautiful eight-pointed stars:

4. Finding the Center of the Square

Draw the square in the method described in section #1. Find the center point by drawing diagonal lines from corner to corner (figure AII-6).

5. Marking Your Reference Points

Position the compass point on corner A with the pencil placed at the square's center point. Set the compass at

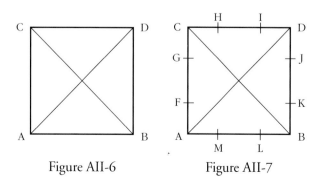

Figure AII-6   Figure AII-7   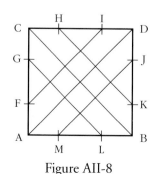   Figure AII-8   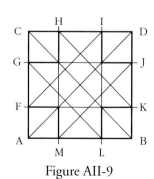   Figure AII-9

this length. This compass setting is the exact distance of your star point markings from each corner point.

Place the compass point on corner A. Make a mark on line AB at point L. (This is the exact distance from corner point A to the center point.) Then swing the compass to line AC and mark point G. You have just made two star points (figure AII-7).

Next, move the compass to corner B. From that position, mark points M and J with the compass. Then go to corner C, marking star points F and I on line AC and CD. Make the last star point markings, H and K, from corner D. After you have marked these two points from each corner spot, the eight star points will have been made.

6. Drawing the Basic Reference Lines

Draw four lines connecting each corner's partner star points: line LG, line MJ, line FI, and line HK. These four lines join the two diagonal lines AD and BC (figure AII-8).

7. Completing the Star

Draw vertical and horizontal lines between opposite-facing star points: lines HM, IL, GJ, and FK. A basic eight-pointed star design is apparent after placing these lines in the square (figure AII-9).

8. Using the Basic Reference Lines in Your Square, Draw Your Pattern

Draw any extra lines your pattern needs (e.g., vertical and horizontal lines going through the center point).

After your design has been drawn, erase all unnecessary drafting lines. Choose the most accurate elements to use for tracing your template patterns from.

9. Eight-Pointed Star Patterns

Below are four eight-pointed star patterns that have wonderful potential for showing depth, shadows, and highlights. There are two other eight-pointed star designs to choose from in Chapter 11, "Patterns," that can be used to achieve other illusions.

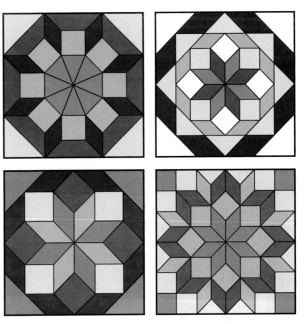

Value changes indicate traditional fabric or color family changes. Clockwise from upper left: Castle Wall, Star and Chains, Dutch Rose, Rolling Star.

"Content itself may be anything. It may be humble or intimate, perhaps only contemplative . . . or it may strive toward the most exhalted in idea or emotion. In such an initial theme lies the cue, the point of departure. But from that point, from the setting of theme, the development of form must be a penetration of inner relationship, a constant elimination of non-pertinent matter both of content and of shape."

—Ben Shahn
American painter, 1898–1969
The Shape of Content

APPENDIX III:

BIBLIOGRAPHY

Birren, Faber. *Light, Color, & Environment.* New York: Van Nostrand Reinhold Company, 1982.

Blockley, John. *Getting Started in Watercolor.* Cincinnati: North Light Books, 1988.

Bonafoux, Pascal. *The Impressionists, Portraits and Confidences.* New York: Rizzoli International Publications, Inc., 1986

Coulin, Claudius. *Step-By-Step Perspective Drawing for Architects, Draftsmen, and Designers.* New York: Van Nostrand Reinhold Company, 1982

Crawshaw, Alwyn. *How To Sketch.* Tucson, Arizona: HP Books, 1985.

DeFiore, Gaspare. *Drawing With Color and Imagination.* New York: Watson-Guptill Publications, 1983. Translated from Italian by Joachim Neugroschel.

DeGrandis, Luigina. *Theory and Use of Color.* New York: Harry N. Abrams, Incorporated, Publishers, 1986. Translated by John Gilbert.

Freedgood, Lillian. *Great Artists of America.* New York: Thomas Y. Crowell Company, 1963.

Gallant, Roy A. *Rainbows, Mirages & Sundogs: The Sky as a Source of Wonder.* New York: Macmillan Publishing Company, 1987.

Graves, Maitland. *The Art of Color and Design.* New York: McGraw-Hill, 1941.

Jaxtheimer, Bodo W. *How To Paint and Draw.* London: Thames and Hudson, 1982.

Lambert, Patricia, Barbara Staepelaere, Mary Fry. *Color and Fiber.* West Chester, Pennsylvania: Schiffler Publishing Company Limited, 1986.

Linn, Charles F. *The Golden Mean.* New York: Doubleday & Company, Incorporated, 1974.

Malla, Dorothee L. *The Language of Color.* New York: Warner Books, 1972.

Martin, Judy. *Dynamic Color Drawing.* Cincinnati, Ohio: North Light Books, 1989.

McGuire, S.H. *Keys To Perspective: Fundamentals of Perspective in Theory and Practical Application.* Cleveland: American Greetings Corporation, 1972.

Minnaert, M. *The Nature of Light & Color.* New York: Dover Publications, Inc., 1954.

Perry, Patricia, editor. *The Vogue Sewing Book.* New York: Butterick Division, American Can Company, 1970.

Poskas, Peter and J.J. Smith. *The Illuminated Landscape: Defining and Painting Light and Space.* New York: Watson-Guptill Publications, 1987.

Powell, William. *The World of Color and How To Use It.* Tustin, California: Walter Foster Publications, 1984.

Quiller, Stephen and Barbara Whipple. *Water Media: Processes & Possibilities.* New York: Watson, Guptill Publication, 1986.

Sargent, Walter. *The Enjoyment and Use of Color.* New York: Dover Publications, Inc., 1964.

Shahn, Ben. *The Shape of Content.* Cambridge, Massachusetts: Harvard University Press, 1963.

Simon, Hilda. *The Magic Of Color.* New York: Lee & Shepard Books, 1981.

_____ *Sight & Seeing—A World of Light & Color.* New York: Philomel Books, 1983.

_____ *The Splendor of Iridescence: Structural Colors in the Animal World.* New York: Dodd, Mead, & Company, 1971.

Smith, Ray. *How To Draw and Paint What You See.* New York: Alfred A. Knopf, 1988.

Taylor, Barbara. *Bouncing and Bending Light.* New York City: Franklin Watts, Inc., 1990.

Thomas, Denis. *The Impressionists.* London: The Hamlyn Publishing Group Limited, 1980.

Walker, Morton. *The Power of Color.* Garden City, New York: Avery Publishing Company, Incorporated, 1991.

Whyman, Kathryn. *Rainbows To Lasers.* New York: Gloucester Press, 1989.

Williamson, Samuel and Herman Cummins. *Light and Color in Nature and Art.* New York: John Waley and Sons, Incorporated, 1983.

Wolfrom, Joen. *Landscapes & Illusions.* Lafayette, California: C & T Publishing, 1990.

Editorial Advice of Chicago University Faculty. *Compton's Encyclopedia.* Chicago: Compton's Learning Company, 1986.

Suggested Reading List and Study Sources:

Beyer, Jinny. *Patchwork Patterns*. McLean, Virginia: EPM Publications, Inc., 1979 (traditional block designs).

_____ *The Quilter's Album of Blocks and Borders*. McLean, Virginia: EPM Publications, Inc., 1980.

Gerdts, William H. *American Impressionism*. New York: Cross River Press, 1984.

Kelder, Diane. *The Great Book of French Impressionism*. New York: Artabras Publishers, 1980.

Leman, Bonnie and Judy Martin. *Taking the Math Out of Making Patchwork Quilts*. Wheatridge, Colorado: Moon Over the Mountain Publications, 1981.

Mills, Susan Winter. *849 Traditional Patchwork Patterns: A Pictorial Handbook*. New York: Dover Publications, Inc., 1989.

Stuckey, Charles F. *Monet, A Retrospective*. New York: Park Lane, 1985.

Periodicals

American Quilter, American Quilter's Society, Division of Schroeder Publishing Co., Inc., 5801 Kentucky Dam Road, Paducah, Kentucky 42001.

Quilter's Newsletter Magazine, Leman Publications, Inc., Box 394, Wheatridge, Colorado 80034.

Fine Quilting Books from C&T Publishing

An Amish Adventure, Roberta Horton

Appliqué 12 Easy Ways!, Elly Sienkiewicz

The Art of Silk Ribbon Embroidery, Judith Montano

Baltimore Album Quilts, Historic Notes and Antique Patterns, Elly Sienkiewicz

Baltimore Beauties and Beyond (2 Volumes), Elly Sienkiewicz

Boston Commons Quilt, Blanche Young and Helen Young Frost

Calico and Beyond, Roberta Horton

A Celebration of Hearts, Jean Wells and Marina Anderson

Christmas Traditions From the Heart, Margaret Peters

Crazy Quilt Handbook, Judith Montano

Crazy Quilt Odyssey, Judith Montano

Crosspatch, Pepper Cory

Design a Baltimore Album Quilt!, Elly Sienkiewicz

Fans, Jean Wells

Fine Feathers, Marianne Fons

Flying Geese Quilt, Blanche Young and Helen Young Frost

Friendship's Offering, Susan McKelvey

Happy Trails, Pepper Cory

Heirloom Machine Quilting, Harriet Hargrave

Imagery on Fabric, Jean Ray Laury

Irish Chain Quilt, Blanche Young and Helen Young Frost

Isometric Perspective, Katie Pasquini-Masopust

Landscapes & Illusions, Joen Wolfrom

Let's Make Waves, Marianne Fons and Liz Porter

Light and Shadows, Susan McKelvey

Mariner's Compass, Judy Mathieson

Mastering Machine Appliqué, Harriet Hargrave

Memorabilia Quilting, Jean Wells

New Lone Star Handbook, Blanche Young and Helen Young Frost

Perfect Pineapples, Jane Hall and Dixie Haywood

Picture This, Jean Wells and Marina Anderson

Plaids and Stripes, Roberta Horton

PQME Series: Milky Way Quilt, Jean Wells

PQME Series: Nine-Patch Quilt, Jean Wells

PQME Series: Pinwheel Quilt, Jean Wells

PQME Series: Stars & Hearts Quilt, Jean Wells

Quilting Designs from Antique Quilts, Pepper Cory

Quilting Designs from the Amish, Pepper Cory

Story Quilts, Mary Mashuta

Trip Around the World Quilts, Blanche Young and Helen Young Frost

Visions: The Art of the Quilt, Quilt San Diego

Visions: Quilts of a New Decade, Quilt San Diego

Working in Miniature, Becky Schaefer

Wearable Art for Real People, Mary Mashuta

3 Dimensional Design, Katie Pasquini

For more information write for a free catalog from
C & T Publishing
P.O. Box 1456
Lafayette, CA 94549
(1-800-284-1114)

About the Author

Joen Wolfrom has been an educator for over twenty years. She spent the first decade of her career in public school education; the remaining time has been spent in the field of quilt and textile art. Her areas of specialty in public education included individualizing instruction for elementary students, teaching learning disabled students, creating individualized and gifted educational programs, teaching and consulting in gifted education, and teaching upper-elementary students.

Joen became interested in quiltmaking prior to quilting's new-found popularity during the American Bicentennial era. In the early 1980s she developed two diverse piecing techniques that are now widely used in fabric designs—landscape strip piecing and abstract curved designs (curves on the whole). Her use of color and her innovative techniques have attracted wide interest from both people in the field and art collectors. Her commissioned textile artworks and quilts are in private, public, and corporate collections throughout the world.

Since receiving her first national and international invitations to teach color and design classes in 1984, Joen has been traveling extensively, teaching and lecturing in contemporary quilt and textile art techniques, color, design, and other areas of high interest to her.

Joen grew up in a geographically isolated community in southwestern Seattle, set in a woodsy parkland along the shores of Puget Sound. She now resides with her husband and three children on Fox Island, a small rural island off the Gig Harbor Peninsula in Washington State's southern Puget Sound. This pastoral setting offers continual opportunities to observe the colorful beauty of nature often reflected in her art.

Joen's first book, *Landscapes & Illusions: Creating Scenic Imagery with Fabric,* may be purchased at your favorite book store or quilt shop, or it may be ordered through C&T Publishing, 5021 Blum Road, Suite 1, Martinez, California 94553 (1-800-284-1114).

Inquiries about purchasing greeting cards of selected artworks by the author (retail and wholesale) or requests for a current schedule of workshops may be sent to Bon Bluff Images, Inc., 104 Bon Bluff, Fox Island, WA 98333 (please include a long SASE). Inquiries concerning workshop and lecture bookings, or other correspondence, may be sent directly to Joen Wolfrom at the same address.